Rental Housing

DIRECTIONS IN DEVELOPMENT
Finance

Rental Housing

Lessons from International Experience and Policies for Emerging Markets

Ira Gary Peppercorn and Claude Taffin

THE WORLD BANK
Washington, D.C.

Contents

Boxes

Figures

Tables

Foreword

For nearly three decades, the World Bank has been publishing studies and providing guidance in housing finance to the countries that were soliciting for technical or financial support in that area. Housing finance plays a critically important role at the intersection of the broader economy and the financial sector. This theme also brings together many aspects of a country's legal, cultural, financial, economic, and regulatory policies and does so to improve people's lives.

The work that has been done over those years has helped many emerging economies develop their residential mortgage markets, one hopes without exposing their financial systems to undue risks, unlike the recent U.S. subprime crisis. This evolution has enabled more people, notably among middle-income formal sector workers, all over the world to access housing finance and own a home when that goal had previously seemed impossible.

Still, the proportion of the working population in emerging economies that can access finance to invest in housing remains a minority, with adverse consequences on living conditions and the prosperity of many. Access to housing remains one of the most formidable developmental challenges of the 21st century.

Within this context, it is amazing that rental housing as a critical component of any housing policy has remained virtually untouched in most if not all emerging economies, despite being the object of considerable attention and support in most developed economies. Simply said, every country has a segment of the population that cannot afford to buy a home, should not qualify for a mortgage, or simply does not want to own a home at a certain stage in their lives.

The development of residential rental markets also critically depends on the enabling environment of the country (laws, regulations, taxation) and the capacity to raise significant financial resources from investors and financiers. The fiscal treatment of this sector by the public authorities can also play a decisive positive or negative role in expanding (or not) an affordable rental sector.

Since the 1980s when several emerging economies lifted various forms of rental control policies, rental residential markets have remained the orphan child of any comprehensive and affordable housing policy, whereas home ownership has been the object of all the attention, sometimes at the price of stretching the frontiers of accessibility beyond sound financial or fiscal rules. Now the rental sector deserves greater attention and deployed expertise. When properly developed, rental markets can play a formidable role in promoting affordable and decent housing. There are more and more people in emerging economies, and they are living in poor, informal housing conditions. The critical challenge of developing rental markets is getting more important as the world becomes increasingly urbanized and demographic pressures keep increasing the demand for affordable and decent housing. Rental markets also play a key role in enhancing the market value of housing assets and in generating revenues from an unlocked housing wealth.

This book represents one step toward addressing this fundamental issue. As the authors, Ira Peppercorn and Claude Taffin, demonstrate, rental housing comes in a variety of shapes and forms that cuts across all aspects of incomes. In most emerging economies, much of the rental stock is owned by retail investors who manage the units themselves and cannot leverage any form of external finance beyond their own equity. In some major urban centers (for example, Lagos or Nairobi) the majority of inhabitants are informal tenants. This important part of the housing stock and production usually does not receive any form of government subsidies, and the development of these markets unfortunately remains shaped by a hostile or obsolete regulatory framework.

Given this specific situation, there may be no simple strategy for developing the rental sector, along with appropriate financial tools, in a sustainable way. Opportunities exist in most countries to take small, incremental steps that can enable the market for rental housing to grow.

The authors suggest many relevant examples for decisive steps, such as improved landlord-tenant regulations, adjustments to the tax system, simplification of the process by which multifamily properties are registered, or adjustments of the overall system of housing subsidies.

The authors also rightfully note that the priority policy goal for governments should consist of facilitating an environment for rental residential markets to develop, rather than following the older policy approach of governments directly financing, building, and managing rental housing. In the rental sector, subsidies may be deemed necessary to promote decent and affordable housing to targeted parts of the population. In that complex but critical respect, the authors offer extremely valuable analysis of and guidance in the different types of rental subsidies that a government may opt to implement.

We look forward to the dialogue that this book will bring between policy makers, financial executives, regulators, builders, and the tenants themselves. We stand ready and willing to assist those countries around the world that are committed to building their residential rental sectors.

Loïc Chiquier
Director
Middle East and North Africa Region and Capital Markets Global Practice
Financial and Private Sector Development
The World Bank

Preface

The discussion of where people live and how people pay for their housing has undergone a significant shift. Until the mortgage crisis erupted in 2008, the housing policy of most nations focused on increasing home ownership. There had been very little discussion about rental housing, less about social housing, and virtually none about public housing.

The mortgage crisis showed the challenges inherent in pushing for home ownership for all. With homes going into foreclosure and with credit tightening in many countries, the need for rental housing increased dramatically. However, most countries are only beginning to consider supporting rental housing as a shelter option.

The vast majority of rental housing around the world is unsubsidized and in private hands. Everywhere, there is great need for safe, decent, and affordable housing at the lowest income levels. A few countries—mostly developed ones—have a sizable social rental sector, yet even here the demand cannot be met and there are often long waiting lists for subsidized housing in the main cities. In most emerging economies, the only affordable rentals available are in the informal sector, with poor housing conditions and little security of tenure.

This book is an effort to bring rental housing to the forefront of the housing agenda of countries around the world and to provide general guidance for policy makers whose actions can have an effect on where and how people live. It warns of the challenges they face and provides guidelines on how to develop or redevelop a sound rental sector. In doing so, it can enable key players in housing markets—be they government officials, private rental property owners, financiers, or nongovernmental organizations—to add rental housing as a critical housing option and to have an informed discussion on how best to stimulate this sector.

Acknowledgments

We would like to express our deepest gratitude to all of those who have played a role in writing, editing, and publishing this book. Our contributors have brought tremendous breadth and depth by showing their brilliant expertise in so many countries. Thanks to Jan Brzeski, Kyung-Hwan Kim, Yoonhee Kim, Anacláudia Rossbach, and Taimur Samad for their contributions. Thanks also to our peer reviewers, Ellen Hamilton, Olivier Hassler, and Michael Oxley, for their thoughtful comments. Not only did their work make this book stronger, their intellectual and practical contributions to housing have improved the lives of people in many countries. Michel Noel and Simon Walley of the World Bank provided excellent suggestions. Dr. K. S. Yap, Dr. Stephen Malpezzi, and Dr. Ranjith Perera contributed both outstanding academic material and their valuable time to discuss rental housing. Professionals in the World Bank's Urban Sector provided another perspective on rental housing. Thanks, in particular, to Angelica Nunez, Harris Selod, and Victor Vergara. We are grateful to Thelma Ayamel, Sevara Atamuratova, Marilyn Benjamin, and Honglin Li for their administrative support and to Sebastian Molineus, Palarp Jumpasut, and Jamile Ramadan for their excellent help and advice with the publication process. Barbara Hart, Christine Stinson, and Linda Stringer of Publications Professionals provided excellent editorial services. The staff at the World Bank's Office of the Publisher deserves great credit for the design, layout, and publication of the book. Three individuals deserve specific mention: Uloaku Oyewole, who handled many of the publication's internal processes with aplomb; Surachai (Jeff) Fangchanda of GH Bank in Thailand, without whom the Thai interviews would not have been possible; and Lise Lingo, our primary editor from Publications Professionals, who was a model of professionalism, grace, and strength. Finally, the authors are indebted to Loïc Chiquier, Director, Middle East and North Africa Region and Capital Markets Global Practice, who has championed rental housing finance and who has supported this book from concept through publication.

Executive Summary

The discussion of where people live and how people pay for their housing has undergone a significant shift. Until the mortgage crisis erupted in 2008, the housing policy of most nations focused on increasing home ownership. There had been very little discussion about rental housing, less about social housing, and virtually none about public housing.

From a policy perspective, owning a home had been considered intrinsically good. Homeowners built equity, were considered a stable part of the community, and—if homes were financed with a mortgage—provided business for the financial sector. The building and construction sectors also gained. Home ownership was preferred because it was thought to provide owners with security and financial benefits.

Country after country, some formerly communist ones and some developing ones, had tried to jump-start home ownership through ownership incentives and mortgage finance systems. Some countries believed they could skip the steps necessary to build a sound mortgage system and started with a secondary market as a way to push the primary market, creating their version of the U.S. government–sponsored enterprises, Fannie Mae and Freddie Mac. Others originated mortgages in Euros, U.S. dollars, or Swiss francs, rather than in their own currency, because interest rates denominated in foreign currencies were lower, sometimes significantly so. This was especially true in the early 2000s.

To stimulate home ownership, the United States and other countries had encouraged reduced down payments, relaxed mortgage standards, and little documentation. Much of this was driven purely by the private sector and fell outside the sphere of regulatory control, such as no-documentation mortgages and mortgages with many risk factors. These actions contributed to many defaults and to an overall destabilizing of mortgage finance systems in several countries.

Although in all countries a significant percentage of the population lives in rental housing, it had been uncommon for rental to be considered part of a country's national housing strategy. Rental housing was viewed in a negative light, especially if it was owned by the public sector. It could be an expensive budget item, it was cumbersome to manage, and it entailed many legal and regulatory issues.

Not dealing with society's needs for rental housing can have serious implications. In Eastern Europe and Central Asia when home ownership is not possible for some—particularly the young, the mobile, and the poor—people are forced into situations where they have little security of tenure (Brzeski, Dübel, and Hamilton 2006). Because some properties are not formally registered for tax and legal reasons, renters of such properties have far fewer rights than they would in registered properties.

Ignoring the need for rental housing can also keep people in housing that is not habitable, especially in slums. Low-income people, especially those whose income is informal, often are forced to rent substandard housing. If the market could be stimulated to build affordable, decent units, or to improve existing units, then the range of choices would be greater.

What is occurring now is a greater realization that there will always be a percentage of the population that does not own a home, or at least not one financed by a mortgage. In countries where the policies and practices used to stimulate the mortgage sector ultimately created more foreclosures and tightened credit, as occurred in the United States, the need for rental housing will be even greater.

Enabling the development of a healthy formal rental housing sector is important for a number of reasons. First, the rental sector is a natural outlet for those households that do not have sufficient income to afford a home or have not saved enough to meet down-payment requirements. Second, because in many countries, a good percentage of the income earned is informal, there are limits to the share of the population that can qualify for mortgage loans. Third, vibrant rental markets are necessary for workers' mobility. Fourth, home ownership produces greater urban sprawl. This is particularly true as housing prices increase and people are forced to move farther and farther away from the city center.

Issues

Although rental housing is necessary in almost every country, cultural norms, tax codes, and regulations often push it into the informal sector. To create an environment that encourages the rental housing market, governments and regulatory agencies need to address a broad range of issues including assessment of the rental sector, legal and contractual framework, taxation, and subsidies.

Assessment of the Rental Sector

The first priority is for governments to develop sufficient knowledge by performing an assessment of the rental sector. This assessment should include the following aspects:

- Compare household characteristics (age, occupation, income, family type, and size) and housing conditions (location, type of building, size, and equipment of the unit) of tenants and owners

- Discover tenants' reasons for renting (by choice or by constraint) and their type of landlord (individual, real estate company, institutional, public, non-profit, etc.)
- Evaluate the balance between supply and demand (market rent, vacancy rate, etc.)
- Monitor variations in market rent levels
- Evaluate conflicts and the conflict resolution process
- Compare the costs of renting and owning (including obstacles to access to credit)
- Compare rental return and risk with alternative investments (after and before tax) by market segment.

The main data for a basic assessment are available from population census and housing surveys. Adding a few questions for tenants in housing or consumption surveys and gathering market information from real estate agents will be useful. Courts in the major cities should be able to provide data on conflicts.

Legal and Contractual Framework

Actions governments take in the legal and regulatory sector need to create systems that encourage rental properties that are safe and habitable. Governments also need to ensure that the rights of landlords and tenants are balanced and that laws and processes that deal with eviction are fair to both parties, efficient, and transparent. Much of this will have to be done on the state and local levels, although guidance can be given from national governments.

Encouraging the development of standardized contracts will also be beneficial. There should be a list of documents that is part of a rental file. The main items to be included here are (a) the definition and description of the rental unit, (b) the duration and termination of contracts, (c) rent setting and rent increases, (d) procedures for resolving conflicts and stability, and (e) adaptability of legal dispositions.

The system should codify the differences between various forms of rental housing:

- Between the units that are the main residence of a household, to which higher protection should by granted, and other rental accommodation such as holiday homes
- Between housing for one person or a family and housing that is shared
- Between social housing and other rentals.

The right balance is required between the core legislation, which needs to be stable over time, and the rest of the rules, which need to be flexible. Main regulations should be consolidated in a single law, not scattered in several texts, including the civil code. In federal countries and those that have subnational legislatures, a similar balance should be sought between the need to harmonize and the need to adapt to the local context.

A rental contract should specify a fixed period for the rental. The length of this period should be neither too short, in order to give the tenant stability, nor too long, in order to give the landlord some flexibility. It should cover the key issues that are necessary to have a strong, two-party agreement.

Rent Control and Rent Setting

Rent setting and rent increases are key issues. Areas that have had strong rent control systems did so to protect the tenants. However, over time, it became clear that rent control inhibited development and that there were better ways to provide affordable housing that was clearly targeted to particular beneficiaries.

In a permanent system, distinction should be made between four cases:

- New rental units created through construction or conversion: rent should be freely negotiated, rules may be set to avoid "usury rents"
- Units that become vacant for various reasons: in most, rent restrictions should be lifted, although there may be some limits using "reference" or "reasonable" rents
- Renewed leases to existing tenants: indexation can be used in addition to the free rent and the reference-linked rent
- Indexation to an official index or no increase in a lease, if it is a short lease (up to one year in duration).

The decisions concerning one of these rents interact with others. For example, where it is difficult to increase the rent after its initial setting, landlords will try to set the initial rent at the highest possible level.

Conflict Resolution

In order to avoid lengthy and costly legal procedures in the former case, conflict settlement between landlords and tenants should be made easier by the introduction of nonjudicial remedies, such as mediation and arbitration. Mediation aims to end the dispute prior to any legal action by entering into a reconciliation process led by a third party who is trained and who is supposed to be neutral in the dispute. Arbitration is intended to settle the dispute by an arbitral tribunal, an arbitrator, or a panel of arbitrators.

Sometimes these are considered phases one and two in dispute resolution, with the parties agreeing to try mediation first. If the parties do not agree, the process can move to arbitration unless the arbitration is binding. Sometimes judicial appeals are permitted, other times they are not.

A good example of such alternatives to the judicial process is Regie du logement in the Canadian province of Quebec. Specialized entities also exist in France and the United States. They are movements to conflict resolution that are quick, fair, and responsive to local circumstances.

A government designing a housing policy to move properties from the informal sector to the regulated sector must be careful that its initial effort is not punitive. It could consider providing temporary tax exemptions to properties currently in the informal sector and incentives to put the properties into safe, habitable conditions. It might also consider incentives for property improvement.

Tax Issues

From a tax perspective, investment in rental housing needs to be on an even playing field with similar investments. Taxes on rental housing should not penalize a rental housing owner when compared with a commercial real estate owner.

The tax code should ensure that rental real estate does not carry a higher tax burden than other real estate in such elements as allowable deductions and depreciation periods. This will help to ensure that the return, the risk, and the liquidity of the housing investment are comparable. These financial prerequisites should help investors get better access to market finance.

If a country wants to develop or strengthen its rental housing sector, it needs to create a balanced tax framework in line with international practices, using as models the countries that have a large private rental sector, such as Germany, Switzerland, and the United States. National and regional differences should be considered as well, because what works in these Western countries may not work in all countries.

A good tax model should include

- Deductibility of main costs such as maintenance work and interest paid
- Economic depreciation
- Possibility to use losses to offset taxes on other types of income.

Additional measures could be taken temporarily by governments willing to give a strong push to investment in rental housing. This has been the case in Germany and France. Other measures could also be introduced against commitments to provide affordable rental.

A government designing a housing policy to move properties from the informal sector to the regulated sector must be careful that its initial effort is not punitive. It could consider providing temporary tax exemptions to properties currently in the informal sector and incentives to put the properties into safe, habitable conditions. It might also consider incentives for property improvement.

Governments might also see what can be done to encourage the development or strengthening of insurance markets for both owners and tenants. Some of the necessary adjustments should be made through taxation and insurance products.

Finance

Long-term capital is essential in developing a large-scale real estate market. Long-term capital is also helpful to individual owners who would like to purchase or renovate other units. Identifying and establishing ways to stimulate equity for rental properties can be important in filling any financial gap. Rarely does a banking system or a government provide equity capital or long-term debt for investment in multifamily residential rental developments. Even when financing is available, some type of additional subsidy, such as a grant or a tax incentive, is usually needed to reduce the amount of debt and provide investors with an adequate rate of return.

Subsidies

There are two ways to fill the gap between affordable rent and market rent: supply-side subsidies, which bring the cost of housing down to an affordable level, and demand-side subsidies, which provide direct financial support to the tenant.

Supply-Side Subsidies

For supply-side subsidies, questions include whether to subsidize only the cost of construction of housing or to subsidize recurrent costs such as building management and maintenance as well. Up-front subsidies such as grants have an immediate budget impact, whereas tax incentives can be used over a long period. Supply-side subsidies should take into account the data available when tenants begin renting, although accurate information can be difficult to obtain.

Direct up-front subsidies from the federal or national and regional or local governments are probably the simplest and most transparent ones. They also do not create long-term commitments as loan guarantees do, and they reduce the amount of the loan, which is reassuring to the lender. Unfortunately, because of the fiscal situation in many countries and cities, there is pressure to reduce this type of subsidy.

Because supply-side subsidies represent a financial commitment from the government to the owner, governments should obtain social commitments in exchange for their contribution. This generally means income limits on those served combined with lower-than-market rents for an agreed-on period of time. Governments should look at the value of the subsidy in relation to the cost of the social benefits that are achieved. In addition, consideration should be given to what happens after the commitment period expires.

Demand-Side Subsidies

Demand-side subsidies (housing allowances or vouchers) are the most effective way to make rental housing affordable to low-income households. Yet they entail heavy fiscal commitments and require the collection and update of information on beneficiaries. Because demand-side subsidies have less effect on housing supply than supply-side subsidies, both should be used in parallel whenever housing needs remain important.

The amount of direct assistance to low-income tenants should be linked to household income, to the rent, and to the type of household or the family size. The subsidy should be adjusted accordingly, as quickly as possible, especially to compensate for major losses of income (death, illness, unemployment).

The scales should be carefully designed so as to avoid the creation of poverty traps, inflationary effects, and a lack of incentive to adjust the size of the unit to the real needs of households. Keep the scales simple and transparent, so that beneficiaries understand how they are calculated.

Combining Supply- and Demand-Side Subsidies

In general, serving the lowest-income groups through supply-side mechanisms only is difficult. Additional subsidies will be needed, such as vouchers, housing allowances, subsidies paid to the landlord, or ongoing payments for maintenance, management, and capital improvements.

Housing allowances and supply-side subsidies can be used in parallel, especially in countries where housing needs remain important. Local or national governments that consider introducing housing allowances should also be aware of the heavy fiscal commitments entailed and of the prerequisite that the administration be able to collect and update relevant information on households' composition and income. Those looking at supply-side subsidies alone or considering building public rental housing should be aware that such efforts are often not enough to make housing affordable to the lowest-income groups and are likely to entail long-term budgetary obligations. The cost and effect of subsidies should also be considered when the owner is a public housing authority, another type of governmental entity, or a nongovernmental organization.

Hidden or unpredictable subsidies, such as interest-rate subsidies, should be avoided, and transparent and measurable subsidies should be preferred. Subsidies that create long-term liabilities should be used with care: when a government guarantees loans, the risk should be measured and limited by strict financial control of the beneficiaries. Whether full or partial guarantees, they should be valued at their actuarial value and included in the fiscal budget. Unless there is complete commitment from the government, which is rarely granted, owners take the risk that incentives will stop at some point in the future. The question then is should other contributors—such as state and local governments, foundations, or employers—be sought?

These are just a few of the key points that will be made in this book. Developing a rental housing market is a matter of putting the key building blocks in place that will take into account the current status in a particular country or region, the needs of the people in that area, the budget the governments have available, and an accurate assessment of what is possible.

References

Brzeski, W. Jan, Hans-Joachim Dübel, and Ellen Hamilton. 2006. "Rental Choice and Housing Policy Realignment in Transition: Post-Privatization Challenges in the Europe and Central Asia Region." Policy Research Working Paper 3884, World Bank, Washington, DC.

UN-HABITAT (United Nations Human Settlements Programme). 2003. *Rental Housing: An Essential Option for the Urban Poor in Developing Countries.* Nairobi: UN-HABITAT.

Abbreviations

ANAH	Agence Nationale de l'Habitat (National Agency for Habitat, France)
ARA	Asumisen Rahoitus Ja Kehittämiskeskus (Housing Finance and Development Centre, Finland)
BGK	Bank Gospodarstwa Krajowego (Poland)
CDC	Caisse des Dépôts et Consignations (Deposits and Consignment Fund, France)
CFV	Centraal Fonds Volkshuisvesting (Central Fund for Social Housing, Netherlands)
CPF	Central Provident Fund (Singapore)
CVG	capital growth
CVM	Comissão de Valores Mobiliários (Securitization Commission, Brazil)
CODI	Community Organizations Development Institute (Thailand)
CONAVI	Comisión Nacional de Vivienda (National Housing Commission, Mexico)
CREDIMAT	crédito para materiales (credit for materials, Uruguay)
Destatis	Statistischen Bundesamtes (Federal Statistical Office, Germany)
DF	Federal District (Mexico)
ENIGH	National Survey of Household Income and Expenditure (Mexico)
ESH	entreprises sociales pour l'habitat (Social Enterprise for Housing, France)
Fannie Mae	Federal National Mortgage Association (United States)
FHA	Federal Housing Administration (United States)
FMR	fair market rent
FNVyU	Fondo Nacional de Vivienda y Urbanización (National Fund for Housing and Urbanization, Uruguay)
FOVISSSTE	Fondo de la Vivienda del Instituto de Seguridad y Servicios Sociales de los Trabajadores del Estado (Housing Fund for Public Sector Workers, Mexico)

Freddie Mac	Federal Home Loan Mortgage Corporation (United States)
FSL	Fonds de Solidarité Logement
GDP	gross domestic product
GdW	Bundesverband deutscher Wohnungsunternehmen e.V und Immobilienunternehmen (Federal Union of German Housing and Real Estate Associations, Germany)
GH Bank	Government Housing Bank (Thailand)
GRL	garantie des risques locatifs (Guarantee for Rental Risks, France)
GST	goods and services tax (Singapore)
HCGF	Housing Credit Guarantee Fund (Republic of Korea)
HDB	Housing and Development Board (Singapore)
HFA	housing finance agency (United States)
HLM	habitation à loyer modéré (moderate rent housing, France)
HOA	homeowner association (Russian Federation)
HOPE	Housing Opportunities for People Everywhere (United States)
HOS	Home Ownership Scheme (Singapore)
HUD	Department of Housing and Urban Development (United States)
IETU	impuesto empresarial a tasa unica (flat-rate corporate tax, Mexico)
INCR	income return
INFONAVIT	Instituto del Fondo Nacional de la Vivienda para los Trabajadores (Housing Fund for Private Sector Workers, Mexico)
INSEE	Institute National de la Statistique et des Etudes Economiques (France)
IPD	Investment Property Databank
ISAI	impuesto sobre adquisición de inmuebles (transfer tax, Mexico)
IVA	impuesto al valor agregado (value-added tax, Mexico)
LIHTC	low-income housing tax credit (United States)
MCMV	Minha Casa, Minha Vida (Brazil)
MVOTMA	Ministerio de Ordenamiento Territorial y Medio Ambiente (Ministry of Environment, Land, and Water, Uruguay)
NGO	nongovernmental organization
NHA	National Housing Authority (Thailand)
NHF	National Housing Fund (Republic of Korea)
OPH	offices publics de l'habitat
PAR	Programa de Arrendamento Residencial (Residential Leasing Program, Brazil)

PHA	public housing authority (United States)
PIR	price-to-income ratio
PIT	personal income tax (Poland, Russian Federation)
PLS	Social Rental Loan (Prêt Locatif Social, France)
PNAD	Pesquisa Nacional por Amostra de Domicílios
PSLA	Social Loan for Rent-to-Own (Prêt Social de Location-Accession, France)
REIT	real estate investment trust
SECOVI	Real Estate Association in São Paulo
SEM	société d'economie mixte (mixed economy company, France)
SHF	Sociedad Hipotecaria Federal (Mexico)
SIBOR	Singapore Interbank Offered Rate (Singapore)
SOFOL	Sociedad Financiera de Objeto Limitado (Limited Purpose Financial Institution, Mexico)
SOFOM	Sociedad Financiera de Objeto Múltiple (Multiple Purpose Financial Institution, Mexico)
TAPRII	Technical Assistance for Policy Reform II
TBS	Towarzystw Budownictwa Spolecznego (Society for Social Housing, Poland)
TR	total return
UN-HABITAT	United Nations Human Settlements Programme
VAT	value-added tax
WSW	Waarborgfonds Sociale Woningbouwe (Guarantee Fund for Social Housing, Netherlands)

CHAPTER 1

Introduction

What This Book Will Do

This book is an effort to bring rental housing to the forefront of the housing agenda of countries around the world and to provide general guidance for policy makers whose actions can have an effect on where and how people live. It warns of the challenges they face and provides guidelines on how to develop or redevelop a sound rental sector. In doing so, it can enable key players in housing markets, be they government officials, private rental property owners, financiers, or nongovernmental organizations (NGOs), to add rental housing as a critical housing option and to have an informed discussion on how best to stimulate this sector.

Methodology

Our methodology involved a combination of approaches, including a review of published material, primary research through interviews with stakeholders, direct observations of rental housing in selected countries, reviews of housing data (such as through a country's census), and application of the knowledge of housing experts in selected countries. A number of case studies are presented, some from countries where rental development policies have been initiated or are being considered with the support of the World Bank. They were chosen based on the authors' familiarity and the World Bank's experience with the selected countries.

Definitions

"Rental housing" is defined here as property owned by someone other than the resident or by a legal entity for which the resident pays a periodic rent to the owner. In "pure" rental housing schemes, there is no obligation for the owner to sell or for the resident to buy the occupied unit. It is simply a formal or informal agreement between a tenant and a landlord to rent a dwelling for a certain period of time at a predetermined price.

"Social rental housing" is defined as rental accommodation in which the rent is set at a level below market rates to make it affordable for people considered disadvantaged, such as low-income earners, the elderly, the disabled, and migrants. The difference between the market rent and the subsidized rent is sometimes obtained through subsidies to the landlord. In other cases, it is provided by the owner if a religious institution, charity, NGO, or public entity owns the property.

"Public housing" is a form of social housing that is owned by a governmental entity.

"Subsidies" are tools that permit housing to be accessible to those that cannot afford market rents. These can be applied to the provision of housing, "supply side," or to assist with periodic payments, "demand side." Supply-side subsidies include grants, low-interest loans, and tax abatements. Demand-side subsidies include housing assistance payments and vouchers.

"Tenants" are people who rent or lease housing from landlords.

"Owners" range from individuals to institutions that own property they rent or lease to tenants. Types of owners include the following:

- Individual owners of a single rental unit or a small number of units
- House or apartment owners who rent a room in their home
- Companies that provide housing for workers, whether they own the housing or partner with a private landlord
- Medium-scale owners who own from 10 to 100 units
- Institutional owners and investors, for whom the ownership of rental housing is a significant line of business.

"Support services" are provided by companies and individuals who help owners with managing or building and maintaining rental property. Types of support services include:

- Property management companies, if the owners hire this service externally
- Builders, contractors, materials suppliers, utility companies, security firms, and others who provide services to the owners of rental housing.

Rationale for Developing Rental Housing

One reason why rental housing is rarely promoted might be a belief that the only way for a government to encourage its development is to create social housing or public housing, which will entail a host of negative perceptions. Yet, as we will demonstrate, rental housing covers a wide range of markets from corporate executive housing to middle-class apartments, to rooms in a landlord's home for factory workers, to units for former slum dwellers, and many more.

Private sector organizations and government incentives promoting home ownership and mortgage finance have sometimes created unintended consequences. For example, in Mexico, incentives for home purchase through retirement accounts have caused some to purchase homes that lie an hour and one-half or two hours away from their workplace in Mexico City. Homes in the center city are expensive, so for some people these distant homes are the only affordable ones. Over time, some of these units became vacant and abandoned as their owners decided to rent a small unit near their employment to reduce commuting time and transportation costs. The 2010 Population and Housing Census found that 14 percent of the housing stock was composed of abandoned houses.

Creating mortgages that are very flexible can help some families obtain a home. Yet, if the underwriting standards lack discipline, borrowers can end up with mortgages that carry a combination of risk factors: for example, an adjustable-rate mortgage that is resetting, obtained with a very low down payment, with negative amortization, and with improper screening of the borrower's income documentation. This happened in the United States and was a key factor in the creation of the mortgage crisis.

As the UN-HABITAT report recommended "Governments should thus modify the regulatory framework, develop credit programs and other forms of assistance to support housing production, with a view to creating more rental housing and to improve the existing stock" (2003, 3). In other words, public officials should change their attitudes toward current housing policies and try to do something practical to help those members of society who live in rental housing, as well as those who can provide rental housing. The private sector should also support this effort.

Why should a country stimulate its rental housing sector? Rental housing offers numerous benefits:

- Aiding a city in developing or redeveloping its urban core
- Providing shelter to transitional workers and to those who are poor or disabled
- Giving short-term workers flexibility and mobility.

However, building a rental sector creates many challenges, largely because the rental market has multiple players, not all of whom have equal power:

- Tenants fear that they can be exploited. They can be forced to live in poor conditions with little power and could lose their home if they complain.
- Landlords worry that they might have difficulties with tenants that could pose financial and legal challenges, particularly if a tenant damages the unit or does not pay the rent.
- Governments see the costs of subsidies as a concern.
- Housing advocates note that some rental housing units are in poor condition.

Increasing Urbanization

Home ownership can increase urban sprawl. This is particularly true when workers purchase homes far from their workplace. Central cities tend to have high ownership costs, but these costs decrease as the distance to the city center increases. A worker who wants to own a home, whether in Mexico City, New York City, or Paris, often can only afford one that is located a great commuting distance from the city center. Working far from home exacerbates congestion on the roads, contributes to pollution, and adds significant cost and travel time for the workforce. A vibrant rental housing market in the urban core can reduce these problems—and can even help to stimulate the city center itself.

The global trend toward increasing urbanization also pushes markets toward rental housing. In any country, the percentage of people who do not own a home is significantly higher in central cities because land and housing prices are higher there. For example, home ownership rates are as low as 14 percent in Geneva and 12 percent in Berlin (table 1.1). Situations are diverse elsewhere, but most of the time home ownership rates vary considerably between central districts and areas that lie farther from the center, whether technically part of a city or in the suburbs. For example, the overall home ownership rate is 34 percent in New York City but 25 percent in the borough of Manhattan, 45 percent in Queens, and 69 percent in Staten. The latter is close to the U.S. average (Furman Center for Real Estate and Urban Policy 2010). In Paris, the ownership rate in the urban area is 47 percent; it is 33 percent in the city, 43 percent in the close suburbs (first ring), and 60 percent in the second ring.

Table 1.1 Housing Tenure, Selected Countries and Cities
percent

Countries	Owners	Renters	Others	Cities	Owners	Renters	Others
Africa							
Egypt, Arab Rep.	69	31	n.a.	Cairo	37	63	n.a.
South Africa	77	22	2	Johannesburg	55	42	3
Asia							
China	84	16	n.a.	Beijing	59	40	1
India	87	11	3	Bangalore	43	55	2
Thailand	82	18	n.a.	Bangkok	56	40	4
Americas							
Bolivia	60	18	22	Santa Cruz	48	27	25
Brazil	73	17	10	São Paulo	70	20	10
United States	67	33	n.a.	New York	34	66	n.a.
Uruguay	62	17	21	Montevideo	58	23	19
Europe							
France	57	40	3	Paris	48	49	3
Germany	43	57	n.a.	Berlin	12	88	n.a.
Netherlands	57	43	n.a.	Rotterdam	26	49	25
Switzerland	37	63	n.a.	Geneva	14	86	n.a.
United Kingdom	69	31	n.a.	London	58	41	n.a.

Source: UNESCAP, updated by more recent data from EMF, NY University, and national surveys.
Note: n.a. = not applicable.

Worker Mobility

Vibrant rental markets are necessary for workers' mobility. It is much easier and less costly to move when a person is a renter than when he is an owner. Selling a house means high transaction costs including realty fees, transfer taxes, and, potentially, capital gains taxes. Ownership can create disincentives to relocate closer to jobs, becoming a "mobility trap."[1]

In general, when a worker needs to move to take a job in a different city, terminating a lease is easier than selling a home. Imagine a tenant who needs to change his or her place of employment to another city. Thus, rental housing can have an advantage in societies that are going through rapid changes in the structure and localization of employment, as in many transition countries (Brzeski, Dübel, and Hamilton 2006).

Although it is possible, in some cases, to rent the owned home to tenants and to rent a home in the new city, there are practical considerations. The reason for the job move could be because of a poor economy in the current location. This could make the owned home difficult to rent, at least for the amount that is needed for mortgage payments. This could be even more the case in areas where there are a large number of foreclosures.

Family Wealth

Among low-middle-income households in particular, the main residence is usually the largest component of a family's wealth, if the price of the property has appreciated or enough payment has been made toward the principal (assuming that the property value has not declined). Although this wealth might give these households a significantly positive balance sheet, in many cases it exists on paper only, at least until the residence is sold. Equity loans—including second mortgages and reverse mortgages—enable owners to "unlock the housing value," but such products are available in only a limited number of countries. A robust rental sector is thus needed to give households a larger choice for asset investment if funds are available.

As an investment, rental housing generates income that complements other income sources. In some countries it may also be a substitute for insufficient or volatile pension systems, thus becoming a critical element of welfare improvement for the elderly. In other words, owning rental property gives an owner a source of income after retirement—whether in addition to a pension or, possibly, as the sole source.

Affordable Shelter

Finally, rental markets can provide shelter to families who cannot afford a home. The quality of rental units varies as greatly as the population of a country. There are several types of options here: an informal rental unit in poor condition in a slum; a market-rate apartment in good condition that is affordable for service or factory workers; a small multifamily property that a young person rents from a relative; and a shared unit or public housing for an elderly person with very little or no income. The quality of the shelter provided in these units is an important component in understanding where a government should and should not target policies to develop or strengthen a rental housing market.

Note

1. A famous but controversial study that linked ownership and unemployment rates in Europe has been confirmed by U.S. data (Green and Hendershott 1999; Oswald 1999).

References

Brzeski, W. Jan, Hans-Joachim Dübel, and Ellen Hamilton. 2006. "Rental Choice and Housing Policy Realignment in Transition: Post-Privatization Challenges in the Europe and Central Asia Region." Policy Research Working Paper 3884, World Bank, Washington, DC.

Furman Center for Real Estate and Urban Policy. 2010. *State of New York City's Housing and Neighborhoods.* NY: New York University.

Green, Richard K., and Patric H. Hendershott. 1999. "Home Ownership and Unemployment in the US." Wisconsin-Madison CULER Working Paper 99-15, Center for Urban Land Economic Research, University of Wisconsin, Madison, WI.

Oswald, Andrew J. 1999. "The Housing Market and Europe's Unemployment: A Non-Technical Paper." Department of Economics, University of Warwick, U.K. http://individual.utoronto.ca/helderman/Oswald.pdf.

UN-HABITAT (United Nations Human Settlements Programme). 2003. *Rental Housing: An Essential Option for the Urban Poor in Developing Countries.* Nairobi: UN–HABITAT.

CHAPTER 2

The Rental Market and Its Players

Abstract

There are three types of owners: individuals or small-scale owners, institutional investors, and nonprofit or limited-profit providers of social rental housing, including governments. Tenants can either rent a unit formally with a lease, or rent informally with little tenure rights.

Introduction

The two major players in the rental market are owners, who provide the supply, and tenants, who provide the demand. Assessing that supply and demand requires good data, which may be lacking or misleading. In some countries that appear to have very high home ownership rates, for example, the data might be biased, particularly if much of the rental stock is informal. To avoid taxation or tenant-oriented legislation, some properties may be formally listed as owner-occupied when, in reality, they are used for rental housing. Sometimes, too, rental units are classified as "other," or units where both owners and renters live that are considered only owner-occupied housing. Consider also the case of a person who rents a room in a home owned by a relative. So there is a significant likelihood that the statistics undercount rental housing.

The Owners: Understanding the Potential Supply

Who are the owners? Three types of owners are usually distinguished: (a) individuals or small-scale owners, (b) institutional investors, and (c) nonprofit or limited-profit providers of social rental housing, including governments.

Individuals or Small-Scale Owners

The first category is the most numerous in almost all countries: individuals own 70 percent of all rental units in Mexico, more than half in the United States, 67 percent in Germany, and 54 percent in France, including 95 percent of the "private" rental sector. Individuals usually own one or a small number of units;

in many cases, they may rent out a room in their house or an apartment in the same building in which they live.

Informal rental is widespread because many owners keep property "off the books" so that they do not have to pay taxes or endure what they consider burdensome laws and regulations. This is common in many Latin American countries. Others do so because the unit itself is informal, which we see in Sub-Saharan Africa. In some cases, landlords build properties on land where the ownership is not clear and then proceed to rent the units.

Some of these landlords may grow into professional investors, either by accumulating units in different buildings or by purchasing inexpensive properties, some of which may be in poor condition, in undesirable locations, or both. Sometimes the impetus behind the growth is that the owner is already involved in real estate-related activities, especially construction.

If rental owners choose to operate in the formal sector, they often choose the legal form of a small business, a limited liability corporation, or a partnership. They may operate in the formal sector for a number of reasons: their size precludes them from remaining unregistered without raising suspicions, they may get tax incentives, and they may gain access to more formal types of finance. In a World Bank study of six countries in the Europe and Central Asia region, such investors were often found in the more advanced markets—in this study, Poland and Lithuania (Brzeski, Dübel, and Hamilton 2006).

However, growth in property size does not necessarily mean that owners will move into the formal sector. There are many examples of property owners in slums keeping properties in the informal sector, thereby avoiding taxation while retaining greater control over the properties by not being subject to laws that could protect tenants.

Individual owners are, of course, not homogeneous. But if we exclude the extremes, such as slumlords or large-scale owners of formal properties, they have a number of common features:

- They need security. Payment defaults that might be no more than statistical data for a large investor could be a financial disaster for a small investor who owns only one or two units. Because of that possibility, small owners sometimes overestimate the rental risk because they are concerned by the bad stories they have heard.
- Their income from rental properties adds to their cash flow and may make an important contribution to their standards of living.
- They might not formally calculate a rate of return. They are likely to rely on rough estimates, such as the gross rate of the first year. They are also more likely to focus on short-term tax benefits. In fact, they might not even care about rate-of-return calculations at all if they are simply looking for additional income or a long-term sense of security for themselves or their children.
- They see taxation as a highly sensitive issue. Tax laws often discriminate against rental property. Such discrimination is at least partially responsible

for pushing rental housing into the informal sector when tax evasion is possible. It can also cause disinvestment if the taxes cannot be avoided. Regulation is a sensitive issue as well, particularly if an owner has any concern about difficulty evicting a nonpaying tenant.

- They must be able to take possession of the property quickly because many of them rent temporarily. They may need the unit for their own use or that of their children, or because they need to sell. Generally speaking, they need quick—and fair—procedures for resolving problems.

Institutional Owners

In the second category of landlords are medium- and large-scale institutional owners and investors with long-term profit purposes. Residential real estate is a relatively risky and illiquid asset; it may also be a low-return asset. These institutional owners and investors are typically entities that invest in all asset classes. Housing is usually a small share of investors' portfolios, mainly for diversification purposes, and it is often limited to the top-of-the-range part of the market. Moreover, it is not easy to manage: for large holdings, professional management is necessary.

Institutional investors are long-term investors who closely monitor their risk and rate of return. They tend to prefer financial assets, which are easier to manage, or commercial, nonresidential real estate, which they perceive as less risky. Investing in multifamily property makes financing more difficult because the long-term financial products they need do not always exist. When they have residential real estate holdings, it is often for diversification purposes or because the investor has significant real estate expertise. When they invest in residential property, they commonly own a large number of units in one building or in adjacent properties, to benefit from economies of scale. Often, they prefer to target higher-income tenants so as to limit their perceived risks.

In the United States, approximately 30 percent of the residential rental real estate is controlled by large corporate entities. Among these specialized real estate corporations are real estate investment trusts (REITs), which are designed to channel the capital of many investors into the real estate sector (box 2.1).

Social Rental Housing

The third category of landlord for residential rental real estate is social rental housing. Here, the rules are not determined by supply and demand in the market, but by criteria such as maximum income, specific target groups and specific modes of allocation, and, usually, maximum rents. Social rental housing generally serves targeted populations, such as low-income families, the elderly, the disabled, and families that have been relocated because of development or disasters.

Public housing is common in both Western Europe and the United States. It was a favored form of housing in Eastern Bloc countries. However, most public housing in Eastern Europe was transferred or sold to residents in the transition to market-based economies.

Box 2.1 Real Estate Investment Trusts

Under a real estate investment trust (REIT), the investor acquires shares in the trust or shares of companies that invest in real estate. Not only are these products more liquid than direct investments, especially if they are publicly traded securities, but they also allow investors to pool risks. The companies' investments are spread geographically between properties. They also may be spread among real estate products such as housing, commercial, and industrial.

The size of these companies' portfolios can encourage better control of spending and provide broader powers to negotiate contracts. The scale of these investments creates the need for professional property management. Sometimes these services are provided through companies closely related to the REIT; other times this function is contracted to an independent entity.

North America has well-established REITs. Australia; Hong Kong SAR, China; Japan; the Republic of Korea; New Zealand; and Singapore also have established or newly formed REITs. In the European Union, four countries—Belgium, France, Greece, and the Netherlands—have clear, tax-efficient REIT structures in operation. Italy uses a hybrid structure. The two largest economies in the region, Germany and the United Kingdom, introduced tax-transparent REITs in 2007. The Russian Federation and Turkey also have REIT structures.

REITs usually pay the majority of their profits to shareholders and, therefore, are exempt from corporate income tax, so that there is no double taxation of the income to the shareholder. In many cases, REITs focus on commercial, nonresidential real estate. Residential REITs accounted for 13.5 percent of the value of all REITs in the United States in 2007 (Newell and Fischer 2009). By contrast, when rental housing investments benefit from specific tax incentives, some funds are dedicated to rental housing, as in France and the United States.

The level of the governmental entities varies. In the United States, although the costs of building and maintaining public housing come primarily from the federal budget, the management is performed by public housing authorities, which are local entities.

In most emerging economies, public housing is either virtually nonexistent, targeted to housing for civil servants or for members of the armed forces, or is a purely local function. In the few countries that remain deeply involved in social rental housing, primarily in Central and Western Europe, the private sector now plays a dominant role in various forms:

- Nonprofit or limited-profit ad hoc organizations in France, the Netherlands, and the United Kingdom
- Cooperatives in Denmark, Finland, Germany, and Italy
- Individuals and legal entities in the Czech Republic, Germany, and Switzerland.

Local governments may be involved through public-private partnerships, and through the donation of land and infrastructure or through tax abatements. Higher-level governments sometimes provide grants, guarantees, and subsidies.

Increasingly, tenants play a role in the management of social rental housing. In the United Kingdom, a new type of organization, the Arm's Length Management Organization, manages the publicly owned units. A board composed of tenants, members of the local authority, and independent people manages these.

The trend we see in several European countries today is a return to an earlier time in rental housing. This means rental housing ownership by small landlords, nongovernmental organizations (NGOs), and associations instead of the large-scale private and public organizations whose growth started in the 1930s and 1940s. Sometimes a combination of more than one type of management, local government, and not-for-profit organization is used (Czischke and Pittini 2007). In essence, instead of governments building and managing public housing, social housing becomes more integrated into the private marketplace and less concentrated.

As an example, housing companies have developed in Germany since social landlords lost their privileged fiscal status in 1990. Contractual regulation of housing occupies a growing place because of the abundance of private supply on markets that are often not under pressure. This lack of pressure helps avoid the concentration of contractually regulated social housing in the same neighborhood or in the same building. The term of social housing occupancy is usually limited to a few years, instead of the previous 35 years.

The Czech Republic offers another example. To increase the supply of rental housing, there are temporary social contract regulations that complement the development of stable social housing by dedicated organizations run by local governments.

France allows private regulated housing. Under the Prêt Locatif Social (Social Rental Loan, or PLS) scheme, investors get a soft loan for up to 30 years and benefit from a reduced value added tax (VAT) rate. The owner commits to maximum rents and maximum tenant incomes for the term of the loan. Moreover, since 2008, some private rental housing has been contractually regulated by the Agence Nationale pour l'Habitat (National Agency for Housing, or ANAH).[1]

In the United States, the Low-Income Housing Tax Credit (LIHTC) gives a powerful tax incentive to private owners, provided that the property follows guidelines for maximum rent and tenant income for a minimum of 15 years.

These examples show that the three categories of landlords take a multiplicity of approaches to rental investment, ownership, and management. Although there are very different types of investors with their own motivations and economic calculations, the common theme is a move toward a market-based approach, rather than an approach where the government finances and manages public housing. Subsidies and incentives may need to be used in some cases, particularly for low income people.

On one hand, it means that the private investment supply can be deep and should have the potential to cater to a significant portion of demand, thus enabling governments to focus public assistance on the categories that need it most. On the other hand, it implies that, when seeking to stimulate the supply, policy makers must differentiate between very different investors' situations and customize incentives to the various motivations and constraints that drive rental investments. Subsidies need to be assessed based on three criteria: targeting those in need, minimizing financial sector distortions, and compatibility with fiscal stability.

The Tenants: Understanding the Potential Demand

Who are the tenants? Their demographics vary as widely as those of the city or country itself. They can range from a Wall Street banker living in luxury in Manhattan to an elderly, disabled resident living in public housing just a few blocks away, from a corporate executive in Mexico City to a hotel worker sharing a room with four others, from a professional at an NGO in a suburb of Nairobi to a small shopkeeper in an informal rental unit in the Kibera slums of Nairobi. In other words, there is no stereotypical renter.

The rental sector is a natural outlet for households that do not have sufficient income to afford a home, do not have income that is formal enough to qualify for a mortgage, have not saved enough to meet down-payment requirements for ownership, or simply do not want to own a home. In some countries, where the private rental market is small or declining, the interim role played by rental stock is unfilled, and young adults live with their parents for longer than elsewhere (for example, in Italy and Spain). When the economy starts to grow and rental opportunities are created, this situation can change. The *New York Times* noted this change in the U.S. housing market in 2012: "As job growth has begun to accelerate in recent months, young people are starting to move out of their parents' homes or away from shared rooms and into their own rentals" (Rich 2012).

In many countries, such as Mexico and Thailand, many renters are workers who migrate to cities from rural areas in their own country or from another country where wages are lower. While some do indeed purchase homes, others either cannot own or prefer to rent so they can save money to send home. Some even own land or a house in their home community. Their dream is to go back home, and they view living in the city as a temporary situation. Then there are those whose incomes are too low, too informal, or both, to afford a home if a mortgage is necessary for its purchase. Students, who often live in dormitories or in rented apartments with other students, cumulate both reasons for renting: mobility and low income. On the other end of the income spectrum are professionals in urban areas who want to live in the city core and do not want to commit to purchasing a residence because they want to remain mobile.

In developing rental housing markets, it is important to understand that there are many different market segments for both tenant and landlord. There are also different segments of properties depending on the type and location of the units. On the tenant side are both tenants by constraint and tenants by choice. Tenants by constraint make up the greater number:

- Slum dwellers or squatters
- Workers who migrated for employment reasons
- Working families who have no access to credit because they have low or nonexistent credit records owing to insufficient or irregular income
- Defaulted borrowers.

Tenants by choice are usually less numerous:

- Housing starters and other young couples and singles who want to remain mobile
- Middle- and upper-income professionals who do not desire home ownership
- Students
- Empty nesters who want to downsize after their children have grown
- All other persons who, for work or personal reasons, prefer a short-term residence.

When renting an apartment, a room in a boarding house, or even a share of a house, a tenant's considerations vary widely depending on the tenant's income, the formality of the rental unit, and the local laws.

For the professional living in Mexico City, the primary criteria for deciding on a unit to rent are likely to be the location of the unit, the amenities, and the price compared with similar units in the area. There is a great likelihood that the apartment will be in the formal sector, with rights, obligations, and remedies written into a mutually signed, enforceable contract.

For many lower-income renters, the power and financial relationships are quite different. The first concern is simply the ability to find a unit that they can afford. For those at the bottom of the income pyramid, this concern can often put them in a position where they feel that they have no choice but to accept what they can rent, even if that means living in bad conditions.

A second concern has to do with stability of tenure. How easy or difficult is it to evict a tenant? Many factors contribute to the stability of the tenure or lack thereof. The power balance between landlord and tenant is clearly an issue, and much of this has to do with the tenant's income. As the income of the renter increases, and the tenant potentially has a greater range of choices, the power between landlord and tenant comes into more of a balance.

A third concern has to do with the laws, regulations, and norms of the country, or even of the state or locality. Strong landlord-tenant regulations do not always protect the tenant. In some cases, they can harmonize the relationships and balance of power. In other cases, they can cause potential owners to avoid the rental housing sector altogether or to have a rental unit only if it is informal.

Rental Housing • http://dx.doi.org/10.1596/978-0-8213-9655-1

In the United States, Boston, Massachusetts, has strong laws regarding tenant protection. It also has a specialized housing court so that landlord-tenant disputes can be handled through a different channel than that used for other civil disputes. This reduces the amount of time needed to resolve disputes and produces more transparency in the process.

In Mexico City, by contrast, real estate owners believe that the laws, regulations, and administrative processes favor tenants. This perception is so strong that the formal rental sector remains undeveloped. Because the majority of rental units are informal, renters may feel that they have little power. They do not own the unit, have no written agreement, and often feel forced to live in unsafe conditions, fearing that if they complain, they may be evicted.

Tenants in the informal sector, such as slum dwellers and squatters, likely do not have the resources to own a home, or they may have constructed an informal dwelling on land owned by someone else. This population segment has the least resources and lives in unsafe conditions. They can be found in the slums of Mumbai, in informal housing on land owned by utility companies in Thailand, or among the hundreds of thousands in the Kibera slums. These informal dwellings create a complicated situation in which tenants do not have formal property rights but are sometimes protected by local laws. Even though they do not have tenure rights, they often live in the same location for months or years, but it means years of unsafe conditions and insecurity.

Not all those who live in slums are renters, though. According to a recent study of tenants and owner occupiers in the slums of Nairobi and Dakar, most slum dwellers in Nairobi are tenants but most in Dakar are homeowners (table 2.1) (Gulyani, Bassett, and Talukdar 2012). Table 2.1 also shows that tenants in both cities had similar or higher monthly median incomes per capita but lower monthly incomes for the households overall. This is because those who own their own homes tend to have more people in their units than those who are renting. (Gulyani, Bassett, and Talukdar 2012).

In countries where most tenants would prefer to own a home but are not able to, this is because their income is low, cannot be documented, or both. For example, in the United Kingdom, the rental sector is heavily targeted toward people in difficulty. Two-thirds of the tenants in England do not have gainful

Table 2.1 Kenya and Senegal: Demographics and Income, Owner-Occupiers and Tenants

	Nairobi		Dakar	
	Owner-occupiers	Tenants	Owner-occupiers	Tenants
Share of households (%)	8.5	91.5	74.5	25.5
Mean household size (persons)	3.86	2.89	10.5	7.0
Share of single-person households (%)	15.4	28.6	0.9	3.5
Median per capita income (US$/month)	40	40	24	27
Median household income (US$/month)	110	87	218	164

Source: Gulyani, Bassett, and Talukdar 2012.

employment. In France and the Netherlands, more rental units are occupied by middle-income households than in the United Kingdom.

In some countries, there is indeed a relationship between owning, renting, and renting in social housing. In France, 40 percent of homeowners have an income below the median. For renters, the proportion is 58 percent in the private sector and 72 percent in the social sector.

In other countries, there is no or little relationship between these forms of housing. In Germany and Switzerland, there are many tenants by choice and their income distribution is close to that of owners. The data from Latin America do not confirm that tenants are significantly poorer than owners. In Brazil, the income distribution of tenants is very similar to the income profile of all households, showing no exceptional concentration of tenants in any income bracket. In Mexico, households with the lowest income (less than three times the minimum wage) have a 71 percent home ownership rate; those with the highest incomes (more than 15 times the minimum wage) have an 82 percent rate.

No single factor, including income, can determine whether a person is an owner or a renter. It is not necessarily true that an owner will be richer than a tenant. Nor is it necessarily true that a poor family will be renters. What the data on income do not tell us, however, is the condition of the dwelling in which the household lives. In this regard, an owned unit is not necessarily a better unit than a rented one. In fact, it can be worse.

Looking at the various types of renters, the various types of owners, and the types of and conditions of housing, we see solutions that can be designed to ease the challenges—and to do so within budgetary constraints. As we will demonstrate, some solutions can be legal and regulatory in nature, some can be in the form of subsidies, and some can even be in the form of supply. An evaluation of the needs of the types of tenants, a policy decision on which ones to assist, and a determination of financial and other resources are critical elements in determining how best to stimulate rental housing.

Financial Issues

Although housing, at its core, tries to solve a key human challenge of providing shelter, it also involves many business aspects. In countries where housing is or has been considered a human right, the government has played a significant role in the provision of housing. However, providing housing is a very expensive proposition and few countries engage in this practice now.

To build or strengthen a private rental market, we need to understand how and why capital is provided. Capital needs, sources, and requirements vary depending on whether the owner is an individual, a small company, or a large-scale investor. An economic calculus is most important to investors and large-scale owners. It is less important to owners of a small number of properties or units, and even less so to individual owners of one or two properties. For individual owners, an economic calculus is not enough to explain what is considered important, how a potential rental investment is evaluated, or why a particular investment is made. These owners are driven by many factors, such as the need to have additional current income, to build a nest egg for retirement, or to provide a legacy for their children.

In general, a rational investor will make decisions according to three criteria:

- *Total return:* This criterion includes rent collection, less expenses, and capital gain upon resale. The ability to leverage the property and any tax incentives factors into this calculation as well.
- *Risks:* The considerations here are lower-than-expected rent collections, higher maintenance costs, increased capital repairs, and the risk that the property could be affected by overall adverse market conditions.
- *Liquidity:* This criterion depends on the ability to sell the property, which in turn depends on the value of the property, which is contingent on the net income, the "cap rate" (the multiple of net income used in that particular market), and overall market and finance conditions. Overall conditions become particularly important in markets when credit has tightened.

For the institutional investor, a financial analysis of a potential investment in rental housing is the primary determinant in an investment decision. This should be done by analyzing the risk-adjusted rate of return.

The decision process must involve a quantification of the risk of the investment. This is easier to do in markets where there has been a history of rental housing and data can be accessed. It is much more difficult in markets where the data are not accessible. In the latter case, investors will have to develop models that can project and quantify different scenarios. The model would have to show that rental housing produces a higher rate of return than investing in government securities to compensate for the additional risks.

The judgment then becomes how to quantify the risk so that safer and riskier investments can be compared. In a market that has experience with both types of investments, this is a relatively straightforward calculation based on actual performance and risk. In a market where there is little experience, such as in Mexico, this is a matter of judgment. In markets that are less developed, it is more difficult to construct a pure market mechanism in which prices accurately express a risk-based economic equilibrium. Information is not always available, there is little history in the rental market to assess risk, and legal uncertainties exist.

When commercial real estate investors in Mexico City were asked if they would invest in multifamily real estate if the rate of return was adjusted by 2 percent to compensate for the increased risk, the answer was no. When the same question was asked about a 10 percent return differential, the answer was that they would likely consider it.

Risk-adjusted rates of return change over time. In the mid-1990s, the Federal Housing Administration (FHA) in the United States sold the underlying notes on some of its multifamily insured portfolio. In the early sales, the notes sold for well below 50 cents on the dollar. A few years later, the notes were being sold for more than 90 cents. There was another reason for this increase aside from the discounted price that is relevant here: the experience of the investors. Experienced real estate investors purchased the notes after undertaking a thorough due diligence process on the properties themselves. They saw that the properties had significant growth potential if they were repaired, updated, and repositioned. When that occurred, not only did the investors benefit from the rate of return from the difference between the discounted notes and the actual value, they achieved an even higher return from their knowledge of the market and their own experience and investments. Therefore, in addition to the calculation of risk-adjusted rates of return, the experience and knowledge of the investors and their willingness to make additional investments is important.

The Investor's Choice: Rate of Return

Rental housing is an attractive investment only if the after-tax net rate of return compares favorably with that of alternative investments that have similar risk and liquidity. In theory, the benchmark for this type of comparison is the government bond of a frequently used maturity (10–15 years), plus some additional return to compensate for the actual or perceived risk.

The total return is the addition of the rental return and the capital growth. The former can be anticipated, whereas the latter cannot be calculated until a property is sold. The most straightforward estimate of the expected gross rate of return is equal to the expected rent (the market rent) divided by the value of the investment (the purchase or construction price). However, the initial estimated rate of return must be adjusted by the perceived risk.

The expected net rate of return takes into account assumptions about both the fees and the taxes incurred in the purchase and the various expenses linked to the operation of the rented unit: utilities, management and maintenance costs, property taxes, losses caused by vacancies, costs of structural investments during the life of the property, and unpaid rents. Insurance premiums covering these risks can be a factor as well. Legal costs are also a factor, and their amount is adjusted for the ease or difficulty of an eviction, in the landlord's perception, if a tenant does not honor the lease.

The expected after-tax net rate of return takes into account the income or corporate tax, and other taxes on rental income. It usually decreases the rate of return. In some cases, it can increase the rate of return when the investor benefits from tax incentives, such as accelerated depreciation.

Assumptions about future economic conditions, including the rate of inflation, are also used, especially when the real estate investment is considered a refuge. In the case of social housing or rent control, rent increases are tied to some type of index, adding another level of complexity.

These are not just economic assumptions; they are often political as well. Investors will ask, is the government stable? Is there any risk that a regime change will affect rental housing? These risks do not exist only on a national level; they exist at the local level as well. For example, what are the chances that a new administration will raise property taxes, institute rent control, or cut subsidies that can affect the property negatively? By contrast, is it possible that there will be a new factory, a reduction in taxes, or a more favorable calculation of a rental index or subsidies?

The gross rate of return can be calculated and compared ex post for a number of properties and investors, because it depends only on the characteristics of the properties. The after-tax rate cannot, if it is dependent on the other incomes of each investor. In some cases, a property can be segregated into its own corporation, which makes it easier to estimate after-tax rates of return.

For investors using credit, the net rate of return should be modified by replacing the total value of the investment by the equity invested, including mortgage take-out and registration fees, and by withdrawing loan repayment from the rental income. In general, using leverage increases the rate of return if the cost of capital is below the rate of return needed for equity.

For a given asset, capital growth is equal to the variation of its value minus capital expenditure, divided by the value at the beginning of the period. For an asset class, sales, purchases, and developments should be included (box 2.2).

Decisions about portfolio allocation depend on the expected return and risk of a given asset class, the investor's attitude toward risk, and the desired holding period, as well as the capabilities of the particular firm and the need for global portfolio diversification. The questions to address include whether the investor is active or passive. Does he or she value current income or future appreciation? What is the investor's tolerance for risk? How knowledgeable is he or she in this particular market? Does the investor have other businesses that can be used or that can benefit from an investment in rental housing? For example, does the investor have a construction firm that is used for noncommercial properties, a real estate leasing company, or a property management arm?

Individual Investors

Most individuals who invest in rental housing base their decisions on much simpler criteria. These criteria vary from one country to another, if not from one investor to another. Most investors have in mind the rental income, any tax benefits, the potential for appreciation, and the anticipated capital gain. Different investors put different emphases on each component. In Germany, the prospect of an acceptable and secure rate of return is essential, whereas in Australia, the prospect of capital gains is particularly important (Oxley and Haffner 2010). Tax incentives have been used in Germany. They are also used in France for individual investors where they represented in recent years up to two-thirds of developers' sales. In that case, many individuals focus on short-term tax benefits and resell the unit after the minimum rental period (now nine years).

The Individual's Choice: Renting or Buying

Just as for an investor, an individual's rational choice between renting and buying a main residence can be based on an initial calculation. However, there are differences. Investment firms have access to more detailed market information than

Box 2.2 Investment Property Databank

Investment Property Databank (IPD) is an independent company, founded in 1985, that specializes in analyzing real estate markets. IPD has established standards of analysis to measure the performance of portfolios and markets. It has data banks in 20 countries, including one emerging economy, South Africa.

IPD indices promote market transparency and ensure real estate plays its part on the investment stage by

- Providing overall statements of a country's investment property return
- Comparing property returns with other assets
- Identifying trends in major market sectors—retail, office, industrial, or residential—and segments in each country.

Figure B2.2.1 IDP Global Annual Property Index, 2010

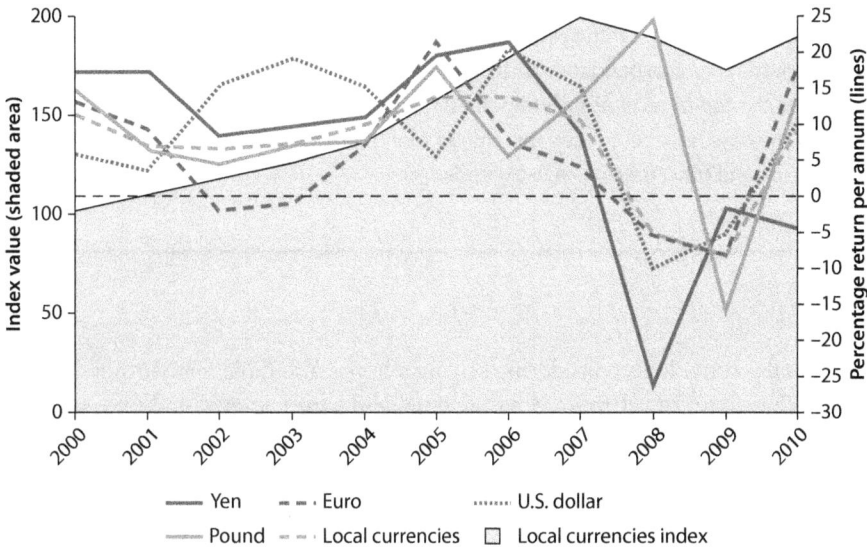

Key IPD Calculations

All IPD measures of performance, including indices, are value-weighted within a single measurement period (the measurement period for IPD performance measures is one month). The values are based on the open-market valuations of each of the real estate assets directly held within contributing portfolios.

Basis of Capital Employed. *Capital employed* is defined as the value of the assets held at the beginning of the computation period plus purchase, development, and other capital expenditure during the period. Capital employed is the denominator of the total return equation.

box continues next page

Box 2.2 Investment Property Databank *(continued)*

Calculation of Principal Single-Period Measures. *Income return* (INCR) is calculated as net income expressed as a percentage of capital employed over the period concerned:

$$INCR_t = 100 * NI_t/(CV_{t-1} + CExp_t)$$

Capital growth (CVG) is calculated as the change in capital value, less any capital expenditure incurred, expressed as a percentage of capital employed over the period concerned:

$$CVG_t = 100 * (CV_t - CV_{t-1} - CExp_t + CRpt_t)/(CV_{t-1} + CExp_t)$$

Total return (TR) is the sum of income return and capital growth. It is calculated as the change in capital value, less any capital expenditure incurred, plus net income, expressed as a percentage of capital employed over the period concerned:

$$TR_t = INCR_t + CVG_t = 100 * (CV_t - CV_{t-1} - CExp_t + CRpt_t + NI_t)/(CV_{t-1} + CExp_t)$$

where

    TR_t is the total return in month t

    CV_t is the capital value at the end of month t

    $CExp_t$ is the capital expenditure (includes purchases and developments) in month t

    $CRpt_t$ is the capital receipts (includes sales) in month t

    NI_t is the day-dated rent receivable during month t, net of property management costs, ground rent, and other irrecoverable expenditure.

Sources: IPD website (http://www1.ipd.com) and IPD index guide.

---

individuals. Individuals considering buying a home also have many other decision factors than rates of return—some financial and some determined by less objective criteria.

For example, in a market experiencing rapid price appreciation, those who might prefer to rent for a period are concerned that they can be closed out of the market if they do not purchase soon. Stories of multiple purchase offers on homes and sellers' unwillingness to accept offers contingent upon financing add to the pressure.

This can work the opposite way as well. Where prices have declined and, especially where many foreclosures have occurred, people are more hesitant to buy. Even if the price of the property is 20 percent less than it was the year before, what is the risk that prices will continue to decline? In addition, price declines are often tied to overall economic conditions. If there is a risk of job loss, a potential buyer may be hesitant. This is due not only to the fear of not being able to pay the mortgage, but also to the possibility that a new job could be found only far from the person's residence. Owning a home could, therefore, reduce the person's flexibility to gain new employment.

Finally, there are factors that cannot be quantified. Cultural norms of home ownership certainly play a factor. So does control over one's life. People often perceive that they have a far greater degree of control over their lives as home-owners than they do as renters. As renters, they can experience rent increases, must deal with a property manager or owner to make repairs, and can be forced to move if the property is sold. If the landlord experiences financial difficulty or if his rate-of-return analysis shows it is not prudent financially to invest in capital repairs or maintenance, the tenant suffers.

Therefore, in many cases, households opt for ownership as soon as they can afford mortgage payments. The first condition is to obtain access to credit. This is often impossible for those whose income is too low or irregular. In emerging economies, such people may be the majority of the population. This is the case in Mexico, where 56 percent of households are informally employed and another 20 percent have a regular but low income with access only to subsidized mortgages (table 2.2).

When lenders fail to follow prudent underwriting standards, disastrous results can occur. This happened during and after the subprime crisis in the United States. In countries where mortgage lending is little developed, many buyers pay the builder-developer in installments, with no guarantee that they will get a property in the end. Often, buyers must provide a down payment upon signing the con-tract. In many cases, they have no alternative because there is no supply of rental housing in the formal sector. This is why rent-to-own schemes have been devel-oped successfully, as in Mexico, for example. During the rental phase, those who pay their rent regularly improve their credit rating and may gain access to credit.

In theory, eliminating the nonfinancial factors, the determination of whether to rent or own can be made by comparing the net present value of the flows of payments between two cases:

- Buying a property and selling it after a given number of years
- Renting a similar unit for the same period.

When making this calculation, the potential tenant or buyer should consider not only the purchase price and the expected capital gain in comparison to the rent and its anticipated rate of increase, but also the following cost elements, when applicable:

Table 2.2 Mexico: Distribution of Households by Type of Employment and Income Level
percent

Minimum wage, multiples	Formal employment	Informal employment	Total
0–3	3.9	16.8	20.7
3–6	16.1	16.9	22.0
6–9	13.1	5.5	18.6
9+	22.7	5.2	27.8
Total	55.7	44.3	100.0

Source: SHF, using ENIGH 2008 data.
Note: Minimum wage equals Mex $1,870 per month, or US$145 in the Federal District for 2012. Formal employment means with access to social security; it refers to the situation of the head of household. This information was available for 24.3 million of 26.7 million households.

For owners:

- Up-front costs including transfer taxes, notary fees, mortgage registration, and real estate agent fees upon purchase and resale for the buyer
- Valuation; mortgage fees; discount points; and insurance, including mortgage insurance, title insurance, and death and disability insurance if the buyer takes a mortgage, and homeowners' insurance regardless of whether the property has a mortgage or not
- Back-end costs, such as realtors' fees and transfer taxes.

For renters:

- Costs linked to the signing and registration of the lease and to the deposit
- Insurance: If available, insurance on the value of the loss of a unit's contents caused by theft or casualty, and temporary location and relocation expenses for a casualty loss; these policies carry lower costs than homeowners' policies because they do not include the replacement cost of the home
- Supply- and demand-side subsidies: Their allocation criteria and amount are different for tenants and home buyers
- Maintenance: Tenants are accountable only for routine maintenance works
- Local taxes: Owners are subject to property tax, and tenants pay no or lower local taxes.

Because the fixed costs linked to a purchase are much higher, the best choice depends on the anticipated length of stay, the amount of up-front costs, the rate of appreciation, and any subsequent sale's costs. The most difficult factor to determine is the rate of appreciation. A study of French data for 2002 also highlights the role of subsidies: compared with renting in the social sector, it takes 10–15 years before ownership becomes profitable; when the rent is in the higher range of the private sector, it takes only 4–5 years.

Small-scale landlords might use risk-adjusted rate-of-return calculations when they consider buying, improving, or investing in rental properties. They consider other factors as well, such as retirement income and financial security for their children. Individual families considering a home purchase versus living in a rental unit might use these calculations, too. However, they often use many other, nonfinancial factors, such as control over one's life, the satisfaction provided by ownership, and long-term stability.

The lack of control in renting can be illustrated through a few examples. When investors who purchased properties for rental before the mortgage crisis did not make payments on the mortgages and lost the properties to default and foreclosure, renters in these properties were evicted. They were forced to move, lost their security deposits and last month's rent, and suffered other financial losses. An individual who decided to rent instead of buy in the metropolitan Washington, DC, area in 1997, when experts were projecting very low property price inflation, would have lost the value of significant price appreciation. Property prices escalated far beyond the early estimates.

Governments considering stimulating rental markets would be well advised to take into account such differences. When dealing with investors, financial considerations—after adjusting for risks—are primary. If a government wants to increase the amount of privately owned, large-scale rental stock, it should consider incentives to boost the rate of return. However, these incentives must be balanced against social considerations regarding the use of public funds for private housing.

For small-scale owners, tax and regulatory considerations are critical. Governments should look at whether their policies keep rental properties out of the formal sector, causing a loss of revenue and less protection for tenants. Sometimes small improvements in property regulation and taxes can produce large gains.

For individuals, one lesson that was learned during the mortgage crisis is that home ownership is not always the best option for everyone. Rental options should be pursued so that families can have a broader range of options in choosing between safe, decent, and affordable rental housing and home ownership.

Market Rent and Price Levels: Where Is the Equilibrium?

Why is the proportion of tenants so high in Switzerland and so low in the United Kingdom? Focusing on the demand side, the answer is that Swiss tenants benefit from better legal protection, including rent controls. Still on the demand side, despite low interest rates, households are dissuaded from buying a home by high prices, stringent mortgage underwriting criteria, and the absence of the tax incentives that are so widespread elsewhere.

On the supply side, Switzerland is an example of a country where institutional investors have a large share of the rental housing market (28 percent). They are willing to invest in residential rental housing because the rate of return is leveraged by low interest rates, with a low rental risk, low vacancy rates, and a weak correlation with financial assets. Federal and local subsidies help match rental yield for investors' returns and tenants' affordability.

Assuming that all stakeholders behave in a rational way, the relationship between the calculations of investors and renters is as follows:

- *Demand side:* To ensure that rental is preferred to ownership, the net present value of the payments made by a tenant in a given period of time must be smaller than those of a home buyer in the same period (see the calculation described earlier).
- *Supply side:* To ensure that there is enough investment in rental housing, the net after-tax rental return on equity must be at least equal to that of the benchmark, such as a liquid government bond plus a risk premium. For this to be accomplished, the minimum rent acceptable to landlords must be affordable to potential tenants. This relation must take account of any supply- and demand-side subsidies.

We have also seen that most households, whether investors or renters, base their decision on other financial criteria:

- *Demand side:* In emerging countries with poorly developed mortgage markets, the criterion is merely the affordability of the mortgage payment, the ability to purchase a home in cash or with seller financing, or the capacity to pay for improvements to a property that is owned. Many households do not have access to credit because their income is informal and difficult to document. They must rely on informal markets.
- *Supply side:* When short-term capital gains are not the main driver, the net (after-tax) rental income—taking into account mortgage payments, if any—should be positive.

Protection for Landlords

In rental housing, both the landlord and the tenant are exposed to a number of risks. On the landlord's side, the risks are that the tenant will not pay the rent or will damage the property, both of which will have a negative impact on the income. On the tenant's side, the risks include the lack of maintenance of the building, the risk of being displaced, and the potential rent increase in the future. Many of these risks depend on the existing and future regulations and the way the landlord complies with them.

Any housing investment is exposed to a number of risks that may affect the value of the property: natural risks such as fires, floods, and storms; risks linked to federal, state, and local legal and regulatory systems; and risks to the macroeconomic environment, to the neighborhood, and to the building itself. In addition to these general risks, a rental investment bears a number of specific risks linked to the rental activity: vacancy risks, the risk of deterioration, and financial risk if the property is financed with an adjustable-rate mortgage. Another critical risk—one that many owners see as the highest risk—has to do with tenants. If tenants do not pay, that lack of income poses both financial and operational risks. If the legal system is cumbersome, time-consuming, or has an uncertain system for eviction, then the investor receives no payment even though the unit is occupied. An owner may also be concerned about tenant damage to the property, which is more likely if the tenant is in a dispute with the landlord. A smaller but still significant risk is damage caused by a departing tenant that may not be covered by the tenant's security deposit.

Deposits

It is customary to require a deposit from a tenant, a lump sum paid upon signing the lease. This security deposit is supposed to be returned to the tenant provided that all rents and utilities have been fully paid and no damage has been done to the property. In the formal sector, the amount of the deposit is usually limited by law to between one and three months' rent. In some jurisdictions, the deposit must be separated from operating accounts and placed in escrow. Depending on local law, any interest earned in these accounts may be given to the tenant. As an additional protection, some landlords ask for an extra month's rent up front; that amount serves as the final payment at the end of the tenant's residency.

In the informal sector, by contrast, landlords sometimes require large deposits—as much as two years of rent. This practice also exists in a few formal markets, such as those in the Islamic Republic of Iran and in Korea. In Korea, the *chonsei* combines rental guarantee and lending between individuals.

This can also happen in the formal sector as well. Real estate owners in the Yucatan, Mexico, noted that they will often ask for a year's payment up front. Landlords also have other means of protection, such as requiring a cosigner or securing rent payments directly through salary deductions.

Screening

Like mortgage lenders, landlords in the formal sector ask potential renters to provide proof of sufficient and regular income, a credit report, and references. Sometimes landlords contract for the services of an outside agent to handle tenant screening. This is especially the case in markets such as New York City, where the competition for rental units can be fierce. By creating strict entry procedures, landlords get the benefit of renting to a tenant who has undergone almost as much screening as a potential borrower for a mortgage. This screening can pose obstacles to tenants with informal income who try to rent in the formal sector.

Public housing often has different procedures for screening from housing in the formal private sector. This is because public housing is heavily weighted toward low-income families, people with disabilities, and the elderly.

Insurance

In addition to the individual guarantees, insurance products have been devised to cover landlords against the various risks identified here. This insurance must take into account the risk that tenants are not properly screened, do not disclose important information such as criminal records, or may act in ways that cannot be predicted. Sometimes adverse events, such as job loss and medical expenses, can affect a tenant's actions.

For example, in the United Kingdom, private companies provide rent guarantee insurance to multifamily landlords. This protects those landlords against a loss of rent through nonpayment. Landlords can also purchase legal assistance insurance to cover the legal costs of evicting a tenant. The recovery payments typically start when the tenant has not paid for a month. Often, the insurance requires the landlord to use a professional service to check a potential tenant's credit.

In France, some insurance companies provide coverage that is limited in time, amount, or both. They require a tenant to have a rent-to-income ratio below 33 percent and a permanent job contract. The cost is in the range of 2.5–3 percent of the total payment, including rent and utilities. It is lower (1.7–2.3 percent) when a professional intermediary manages the unit.

However, most landlords who are individuals prefer to require a third party's guarantee. For units rented to students, that party is typically the student's parents. Because this favors wealthy families, the government has been trying for several years to introduce a subsidized guarantee scheme that would cover tenants without family support.

Under the Garantie des Risques Locatifs (Guarantee for Rental Risks, or GRL) scheme, private landlords may sign such a contract with any participating insurance company for units that are rented for less than €2,000 per month.[2] The payment-to-income ratio (rent plus utilities divided by net income) of the tenant is less than 50 percent. The coverage includes payment default on rent, utilities, and taxes; damage to the unit up to €7,700; and legal costs. When a tenant has an initial payment-to-income ratio of between 28 and 50 percent or belongs to certain categories, such as students, the unemployed, or young workers, the state budget or the employers' fund will pay a subsidy to the insurance company in case of a loss.

In Spain, a public institution (*sociedad pública de alquiler*) has been created to provide guaranteed rental schemes for tenants and landlords in order to encourage the development of the rental sector. It manages the leasing procedure, guarantees the contract arrangements, manages the necessary legal actions if the contract is breached, and provides full management services, including the search for a new unit should the tenant move for employment-related reasons (Andrews, Sanchez, and Johansson 2011).

In Mexico, because the formal rental system is not well developed, such guarantees do not exist on a large scale and their cost is expensive. An informal estimate suggests that all insurance firms combined cover no more than 5 percent of the formal rental stock. Their clients are institutional investors and individuals who have had a bad experience with tenants. These insurance companies sell two products:

- An insurance product that covers any loss from unpaid rent, from damages to the property, or from legal costs, with a maximum of 100 times the monthly rent or up to Mex$5 million annually, whichever is lower. The cost is an annual fee of 110 percent of the monthly rent.
- A factoring product with a limit of Mex$15,000 per month is paid until the landlord recovers the property. The cost is an annual fee of 50–80 percent of the monthly rent.

Both products offer mediation as a first option to avoid a judicial process. According to the manager of one insurance company, the rate of delinquency of one month's payment has decreased from 30 to 5 percent since tenants' defaults began to be reported to the credit bureaus.

Stability of Tenure

In different countries and even within the same country, there are great variances in the stability of tenure. In some cases, the tenant resides completely at the will of the landlord. This is particularly true in informal housing, such as a boarding house or a room in someone's apartment. In these situations there is rarely a lease and the tenant has few, if any, rights. However, there are cultural norms that give both parties stability.

Some situations can create instability or loss of tenure. In a market undergoing gentrification, rent increases are possible if the units are sold. In informal housing, tenants can rent from a landlord who does not have legal title to the property, raising the risk that they may be displaced, either by the government or by the rightful owner, if there is one.

In some cases, landlords keep the tenant's security deposit even if this is not warranted. If a tenant wants to fight a landlord on this issue, it usually requires pursuing legal action. The legal and court costs, as well as the value of the tenant's time, can be greater than the value of the security deposit. For that reason, many tenants choose not to fight for return of the deposit.

In the United States, there is also the possibility that if the landlord defaults on a property, the tenant will not only lose the security deposit but could face eviction when the property is repossessed by the lender. In 2009, the Office of the Comptroller of the Currency established procedures to protect the tenant in these cases. Protections were also added in the Dodd-Frank legislation.

Public housing residents and those with governmental subsidies are not immune from losing their residence. For example, a government may require that a property be torn down because of poor conditions or, in fewer cases, because of development. In the United States, public housing tenants have some degree of protection. In general, the government requires that displaced public housing residents receive a replacement unit or a housing voucher that enables them to find housing in the private market. Although this does indeed give them a place to live, it can create displacement from the neighborhood. Residents who live near their workplace might be forced to live on the other side of a city, creating longer commutes, requiring a move to new schools for their children, and entailing a loss of community.

At times, an owner commits to serve certain classes of tenants or to provide lower-than-market rents in exchange for some type of incentive, be it a tax credit, a grant, a low-interest loan, free or discounted land and infrastructure, or monthly payments to compensate for the difference between the market rent and the rent paid by the tenant. The commitment such owners make is generally for a limited period. When the commitment expires, the owner can convert the property to market-based rents. Tenants are afforded some type of protection, but the relocation issues apply here as well.

Condition

One of the major problems that tenants experience is that landlords rent units that are either in poor condition initially or that they allow them to deteriorate. Such units may be in a slum, in public housing, or even in market-rate, private housing. The risks certainly increase when the tenant has a very low income, especially if the unit is in the informal sector and the tenant does not have a lease. When a unit is in poor condition, the tenant faces the risks not only of displacement, but of health and safety issues as well. Natural disasters such as earthquakes and floods can threaten tenants' lives when a property is not built to a standard of safety.

Dispute Resolution

One of the key issues for security of both tenure and condition is whether or not there is a written contract, which is unlikely in informal rentals. Security may also depend on the physical location of the landlord. A tenant who shares a room in a landlord's house or rents an apartment in the building where the landlord lives is more likely to have a personal relationship with the landlord and, therefore, resolve disputes informally. At the more secure end of the spectrum are long-term leases or leases that, once entered into, can give the tenant strong rights. Informal housing rarely provides an agreement, so the tenure is not secure and the tenant has few rights.

Security of tenure also depends on the country and jurisdiction in which the property is located. Jurisdictions in development markets with formal rental housing likely have far greater legal protections than ones in less developed, informal markets. However, even if the laws are strong, engaging in a legal dispute with an owner is costly, time-consuming, and risks reprisals from landlords.

Creating systems to protect both tenants and owners is not easy. Requiring greater tenant protection may slow investment in rental housing by individual or small owners who worry about the effect of regulations. Potential owners may not invest for fear that if a tenant does not pay the rent, eviction could take a long time. In most countries, dispute resolution is handled through the courts. Typically, there is no guarantee of the timing of the resolution or of the ultimate outcome. Streamlining regulations can certainly help promote investment in rental housing. Rental housing is more attractive as an investment where laws, regulations, and processes are transparent, fair, and timely.

The issue of physical condition is much more difficult to handle, especially in informal housing in developing countries. In many places, there are no housing standards or housing codes. Where they exist, enforcement may be subject to delay or corruption. However, in more and more places around the world, poor housing conditions are being dealt with. The impetus can come from lending institutions that will not lend to an owner with poor construction standards, from a city that insists on housing codes, or from a federal government that constructs housing so that those living in unsafe housing can move to units in good condition. Each government must decide how and when to step in—or whether it has the capacity to step in at all. If a government does engage, it should do so in a way that emphasizes fairness, encourages potential investments, and improves the health and safety of the tenants.

Alternative Tenure Forms

In developed countries and even more in emerging economies, several categories of households cannot access full home ownership of a formal unit. Some have income so low as to make loan repayment too heavy a burden; others have income that is informal and difficult to document. Some do not have the down payments lenders require. Some have no access to credit because they have a minimal or nonexistent credit record. Many face all these challenges.

Potential homeowners are not the only ones who face these challenges. The challenges also can affect those who would like to rent in the formal sector but would have difficulty affording rents, proving income, or demonstrating good credit.

How can access to the first step of the housing ladder be made easier? People may choose to live in units that are too small for the household, that are in an undesirable location, that are in poor condition, that are unregistered, or that have a combination of these factors. Government may provide various kinds of subsidies to make either home ownership or rental more affordable. These are not the only alternatives. Other alternatives explored by organizations in different countries are neither traditional home ownership nor pure rental.

These forms of housing and housing finance are trying to solve the problems of credit, of down payments and deposits, and of the level and formality of income. Often, a third party is involved, such as a governmental agency or an NGO. A distinction should be made between three types of schemes:

- Those that have full ownership as an ultimate aim, such as rent-to-own schemes.
- Those in which shared ownership of the property or the land may continue for a long term. (Usually, more than one unit in a building is owned in common. Sometimes land is owned in common as well. In other cases, the entire property is owned in common.)
- Those that pool the resources of individual members into groups as housing cooperatives. (Not all cooperative housing fits in this category. Some housing cooperatives serve middle- and upper-income people and are more like condominiums than this form of tenure.)

"Rent-to-Own" Schemes

In a rent-to-own scheme, the buyer and the seller sign an agreement in which the seller commits to transfer full ownership of the unit at a future date after a rental phase. Sometimes there is a third party to this agreement, such as a government agency. During the rental phase, which can range from a few months to 15 years or more, the household makes a monthly payment, a portion of which is considered rent and a portion of which is used to build what will ultimately serve as equity. In most cases, the resident must use the option to buy within the period fixed by the contract. Different contracts have different consequences if the tenant fails to do so. In some, the tenant can continue to rent. In others, the tenant might have to leave the property yet receives the funds that were put toward the residence as a down payment. In some, those payments might be forfeited. Those entering into rent-to-own schemes must fully understand the costs and the risks involved.

These schemes may work on a pure market basis, but in many countries, such as Algeria, Brazil, France, and Mexico, they are subsidized, sometimes heavily, at the federal, state, or local levels. In Brazil, the PAR (Programa de Arrendamento Residencial) subsidy was one of the key instruments for housing policies from 2001 to 2009. In France, in the PSLA (Prêt Social de Location-Accession) scheme, potential beneficiaries are income tested. They cumulate the tax benefits of social landlords, including a reduced VAT rate and long-term property tax exemption, and those of first-time buyers, such as a no-interest loan. There is a maximum selling price, which decreases by 1 percent each year. If tenants do not exercise their option, their contributions are fully reimbursed. In Mexico, rent-to-own schemes are the only form of non-home ownership support from the federal government. Rental housing is not supported at any governmental level.

Rent-to-own schemes are sometimes handicapped by the rigidity of the legal system. Tenants must also pay for the management cost of the rental phase. From the developer's or seller's point of view, rent-to-own systems have benefits and costs. For example, such a system might allow them to sell a property that they had been unable to sell, particularly if it enables buyers to finance the purchase when they might not have been able to do so otherwise.

Although these schemes can sometimes be less expensive for tenants, particularly if a subsidy is involved, this is not always the case. Sometimes the long-term costs can be higher than an outright purchase. Moreover, some tenants enter rent-to-own schemes because they think that they would not be eligible for a mortgage, when that is not necessarily the case.

Long-Term Leases, Shared Ownership, and Partial Ownership

In several countries, ownership of land is restricted. In the United Kingdom, according to common law, only the king was entitled to full ownership under freehold tenure. Leasehold tenure provides only an occupancy right with limited time. Nowadays, the leaseholder is usually considered an owner if the lease is for 21 years or more and considered a tenant otherwise.

In several Asian countries, including China, land belongs to the state. Home ownership is thus limited to the building. The land is leased for a period of up to 70 years. There are also countries where the usual rule is full ownership but land may be leased for a long period to make access to home ownership cheaper. In France, land may be leased for up to 99 years.

Some countries have tried to develop original mechanisms with the same purpose of making access cheaper, but using other types of divisions than those between land and buildings. In the Netherlands, *koophuur* (buy-rent) consists of a permanent separation of the property between the inside and the outside of a unit. The household owns only the inside of the unit and is considered a tenant of the rest of the building. It pays a rent that is approximately 35 percent less than the market rent. The owner of the building is a social landlord and remains in charge of the maintenance of the common areas. The owner-occupier of the unit is responsible for maintenance of the unit. The occupier may transfer his right, but he may not lease the premises. Koophuur is therefore closer to a new form of rental than of ownership.

In England, several forms of shared ownership have been introduced since the 1980s: conventional shared ownership, do-it-yourself shared ownership, and, since 1999, Homebuy. These forms do not consist in a physical division of the property. The owner buys shares of the whole property, and a social landlord owns the rest. In the Homebuy, the owner buys 75 percent of the property with a mortgage loan; for the remaining 25 percent, the owner gets an interest-free loan from the landlord. The owner may pay back this loan whenever he or she wants and thus become a full owner. Alternatively, when the property is sold, the landlord gets the corresponding share of the capital gain. The state and the local authorities subsidize this scheme. The size of the program is limited, and it is only available in markets with high demand. It targets low-income households that cannot afford to purchase a unit at the market price.

In Finland, the *asumisoikeus asuminen* (right of occupancy) is designed to help middle-income households acquire an adequate-size home in tight markets. The household pays 15 percent of the acquisition cost. The acquisition cost is increased annually at a rate equivalent to the construction cost index. This is the payment the household receives when it moves out. The property is owned and managed by social landlords.

This right-of-occupancy scheme does not entitle residents to purchase their homes, although the owners of the housing cannot unilaterally terminate the right-of-occupancy agreement. The rent is based on the cost-recovery principle. Just over 1 percent of Finnish households live in right-of-occupancy housing, a figure that can be considered a success because the scheme was introduced only in the beginning of the 1990s.[3]

Apart from the division between land and building ownership, which is the rule in some countries and feasible in others, most of these schemes entail legal and management costs. Therefore, they can work only with heavy subsidies. Few of them have reached a significant size.

Sometimes, though, shared housing solutions develop in the marketplace without the benefit of governmental subsidies. In Boston, Massachusetts, many three-family homes, known as "triple deckers," were built during the early part of the 20th century. In some cases, ownership was shared between different members of the same family who lived on different floors. Sometimes an owner owned all three units, living in one and renting the others to members of the family or to other tenants. The FHA implicitly supports this type of ownership, because properties of four units or less are eligible for single-family mortgage insurance.

Cooperative Housing

Generally speaking, a housing cooperative is an intermediate form of tenure between rental and ownership. The residents are, in a sense, tenants in their own units and owners of a share of the whole building or group of buildings. Cooperatives offer households property rights that are different from those of both tenants and conventional homeowners. In practice, cooperative housing can sometimes be close to home ownership and sometimes to rental. The key difference has to do with restrictions on the sale of the property and on the benefit of property appreciation. In the most common form of rental cooperatives, the tenants pay a low rent (often a cost-price rent) in exchange for investing in the equity of the cooperative. Sometimes this is composed of a maintenance fee and an escrow for property taxes. They have the right to sell their share but not the unit. If the equity is borrowed, the resident will also have mortgage payments.

As a form of ownership, cooperative housing is different from condominiums. In condominiums, residents own their unit; in cooperatives, they own stock or shares of the entire property. In both cases, financial assessments paid by the residents maintain the common areas and systems of the property.

In some cooperatives, residents receive the gain on the sale, less some fee. There are few, if any, restrictions on the purchaser, other than the approval of the board of directors. In such cases, cooperative housing is closer to home ownership.

In other cases, sales are extremely restricted, for example, only to a person in the community on a waiting list. Sometimes there is no gain or appreciation, and the property is simply transferred or the new resident returns the initial equity to the incumbent. When the sellers do not reap the gains, this case is closer to the more secure type of rental housing.

There are middle grounds, too, where a unit can be sold at a market price or at a price that permits partial gains, but only to a buyer who meets the cooperative's eligibility criteria. The cooperative may share in the gain on the sale as well. Here, sellers gain more than they would have in a pure rental unit but less than they would have if they had owned the unit.

Cooperative housing in which the residents are owners is very common in New York City. It started in the early 20th century with new immigrants, particularly from Central and Eastern Europe. Although a board of directors approves any sale or transfer, the vast majority of capital gains on the sale or transfer goes to the seller. Cooperative housing like this can be targeted to moderate-income people, but it also can be targeted to people who can afford a multimillion-dollar residence.

A type of cooperative that is closer to rental housing can be seen in Southeast Asia. In Thailand, the Community Organizations Development Institute (CODI) assists locally based organizations to purchase land or to enter into a long-term lease on land upon which new housing will be built. The residents are very-low-income people, some of whom reside in informal housing built along riverbanks and are at risk when the river floods. They can also be displaced persons. The organization of residents holds the land and the properties in common. When a resident would like to move, the gain on the sale does not go to the seller; it goes to the organization. Moreover, residents must meet strict eligibility requirements and are usually drawn from a waiting list of nearby residents.

The government of Thailand provides significant subsidies. Eligible low-income people may receive B 80,000 for housing. CODI also receives funds from the government that it loans to the cooperatives at interest rates in the range of 2 percent. The cooperative then lends the funds to the families at approximately 4 percent, with the difference going to administrative costs and the costs of social welfare housing.

Cooperative housing is a popular tenure form in Central and Northern Europe. Two-thirds of the cooperative housing units are designated for home ownership and one-third for long-lease contracted units for cooperative members. In Poland, cooperative housing makes up almost 30 percent of the housing stock, with a majority of the properties owned by the residents, although individual units are sometimes informally rented. In the Czech Republic, 17 percent of the stock is managed by rental housing cooperatives (see the country experience cases). In Sweden and Norway, cooperative homeowners own 15–17 percent of the housing stock (Vaníček 2011).

Notes

1. Its main mission is to subsidize the renovation of the private rental stock and of units occupied by low-income owners.
2. Most rents in the private sector are between €10 and €25 per square meter.
3. Information provided by Martti Lujanen, consultant, former director-general at the Ministry of the Environment, Finland.

References

Andrews, Dan, Aida Caldera Sanchez, and Asa Johansson. 2011. "Housing Markets and Structural Policies in OECD Countries." OECD Economics Department Working Paper 836, OECD Publishings, Paris. http://dx.doi.org/10.1787/5kgk8t2k9vf3-en.

Brzeski, W. Jan, Hans-Joachim Dübel, and Ellen Hamilton. 2006. "Rental Choice and Housing Policy Realignment in Transition: Post-Privatization Challenges in the Europe and Central Asia Region." Policy Research Working Paper 3884, World Bank, Washington, DC.

Czischke, Darinka, and Alice Pittini. 2007. *Housing Europe 2007, Review of Social, Cooperative and Public Housing in the 27 EU Member States.* Brussels: CECODHAS European Social Housing Observatory.

Gulyani, Sumila, Ellen M. Bassett, and Debrabata Talukdar. 2012. "Living Conditions, Rents, and Their Determinants in the Slums of Nairobi and Dakar." *Land Economics* 88 (2): 251–74.

IPD (Investment Property Databank). http://www1.ipd.com.

Newell, Graeme, and Franz Fischer. 2009. "The Role of Residential REITS in REIT Portfolios." *Journal of Real Estate Portfolio Management* 15 (2): 129–39.

Oxley, Michael, and Marietta Haffner. 2010. "Housing Taxation and Subsidies: International Comparisons and the Options for Reform." Joseph Rowntree Foundation, York, U.K.

Rich, Motoko. 2012. "Rents Keep Rising, Even as Housing Prices Fall." *New York Times*, February 25. http://www.nytimes.com/2012/02/25/business/homes-arent-selling-but-its-an-apartment-landlords-market.html?_r=2&pagewanted=all.

SHF (Sociedad Hipotecaria Federal) using ENIGH 2008 data.

Vaníček, Vít. 2011. "Housing Cooperatives and Housing Markets in Europe." Paper presented at CECODHAS Housing Europe, Torino, February 23–24.

CHAPTER 3

Legal, Tax, and Financial Issues

Abstract

Legal, tax, and financial issues pose different challenges in different countries. They arise in connection with landlord-tenant relationships, incentives for both tenants and investors, and the provision of financing and subsidies—an important issue in its own right.

Legal Issues

The cultural differences between countries are reflected in (and perhaps caused by) their legal systems. Ironically, those countries with the strongest negative attitudes toward rental housing are often the most protective of tenants. This contradiction creates a vicious cycle whereby those who might consider investing in rental housing might be hesitant to do so because of fears that the legal system will protect tenants who do not pay rent for months or years. In some countries, even if a landlord wins a positive decision in court, the municipal jurisdiction might avoid carrying out the court order. All the while, the owner loses money and damage may be done to the unit. Casa-Arce and Saiz (2007) showed that in countries with less efficient contract enforcement and less fair judicial systems, the share of rental housing is substantially smaller.

By contrast, among countries under study, developers and owners in Thailand have a positive attitude. It is expected, both legally and culturally, that a tenant will pay the rent. If a tenant does not, the landlord can simply change the lock or padlock the door. Landlords in Bangkok expressed none of the fears that builders in Mexico did about tenants not honoring their responsibility to pay the rent and about being tied up for months or years in the court system.

Neither of these examples is meant to imply that laws and regulations should not be created. In fact, many laws protecting tenants were created because tenants needed protection. Historically, laws favorable to tenants were introduced because the 19th century was marked by landlord mistreatment of tenants. The name of one such landlord, Charles Boycott, was infamous enough to enter the dictionary. "Boycotts" were organized against him by Irish tenants who felt mistreated.[1]

Developing rental markets requires a number of actions to protect both landlords and tenants. These actions are efficient only if they are all taken and in a systematic order. Most often, improving the legal framework is the first priority. It is also time-consuming and difficult, from both a technical and a political point of view. Changing legal dispositions that are often embedded in the civil code, whether at the federal, state, or local level, is a great challenge.

Rental Regulation and Supervision

In most centralized countries, such as France, Italy, and the United Kingdom, the core rental regulation is handled at the national level. In federal countries, such as Germany, India, Mexico, and the United States, a variety of situations are found. In Germany, the core regulations are at the federal level. More frequently, rental regulation and supervision is handled at the municipal or state level, not at the federal level. However, federal governments can set standards that local zoning, planning, and housing agencies could follow. The federal government can also legislate that certain issues be part of local codes, even if the precise way this will be handled is left to the municipal or state governments. Rental contracts themselves are legal documents. Local or state legislatures could define what must be in the contract. The courts would then have the responsibility for adjudicating a dispute in the case that either party does not follow a contract.

Another critical issue is the condition of the unit. The starting point should be the development of health and safety standards. Although the terms "safe and decent" are often used to describe what housing should be, decent is not always easy to define. However, the development of international health and safety standards should be encouraged. Whereas an international body would not have enforcement powers, it could set the guidelines by which governments should set the standards and develop the mechanisms for enforcement.

There is no question that there will be pushback on the issue of standards for decent housing. Some will argue that such standards would increase costs in rental housing and either make it unaffordable for some, cause disinvestment, or increase the number of informal, unregulated units. Local governments could also complain that they do not have the funds or the expertise to monitor rental units effectively. This argument would be particularly strong in developing countries.

Although these arguments are understandable, failure to adopt or enforce health and safety standards can endanger people's lives, whereas having strong standards can save them. Consider, for example, the difference in loss of life after the earthquakes in Haiti, where much of the housing was informal and unregulated, and in Chile, where building standards were much stronger. These benefits apply to owner-occupied housing as well, of course.

Rent Control Guidelines and Market Forces

Although rent controls are favored by some as a way to protect tenants, they are another part of the legal system that may deter investors from the rental

Figure 3.1 England: Privately Renting Households

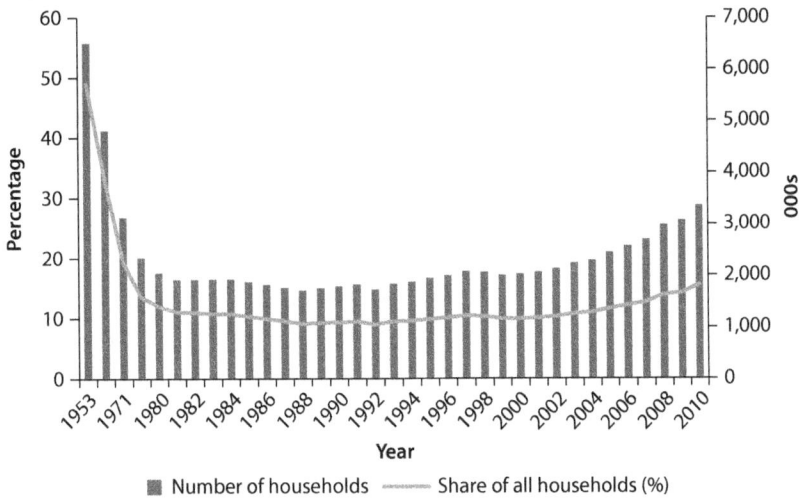

Source: Based on Kemp 2008.

sector for decades. Owners may stop both investment and maintenance of rent-controlled units. This was a significant factor in the reduction of private rental housing from 50 to 10 percent of the housing stock in England in the second half of the 20th century (figure 3.1). This also happened in most of Western Europe and all around the Mediterranean Sea. The ending of hard rent controls occurred more recently in Southern Europe and is still under way in countries in the Middle East and North Africa such as Jordan, Lebanon, and Morocco.

Filling the gap between the very low controlled rents and the market-level ones, even by spreading increases over several years, is hardly possible when tenants' incomes are stagnating and governments are unable to contribute.

Rent control can be considered a subsidy to the tenant paid by the landlord. If a government chooses to end an existing rent control scheme, it must be prepared to have systems in place to protect tenants from sharp increases. It might also have to prepare for increased budgetary costs as this social protection moves from the private sector to the government.

Few countries have moved away from excessive tenant protection as sharply as the United Kingdom. Countries that want to phase out rent control often proceed gradually. Usually, rent control on the existing stock is maintained, while new construction is exempted from it. This creates a dual rental market, with very low rents in the rent-controlled segment and very high rents for uncontrolled units. Table 3.1 provides an overview of practices in the European Union.

There are many alternatives to full rent control, including the following examples:

Table 3.1 European Union: Private Rent Setting, Main Options

	Newly rented	*New tenancy*	*Existing leases*
Austria	Yes, if subsidized	Yes, if pre-1953 or subsidized	Yes, CPI
Belgium	No	No	Yes
Denmark	Yes, for pre-1991 buildings	Yes, for pre-1991 buildings	Lease must specify or CPI
Finland	No	No	Yes
France	No	No	Yes
Germany	Yes, if subsidized; usury law applies	Yes, if subsidized; usury law applies	Yes, not more than 20% in 3 years
Ireland	No	Yes, must be "market rent"	Yes
Netherlands	Yes, based on points system	Yes, based on points system	Yes, CPI
Spain	No	Yes	Yes, CPI
Sweden	Rents cannot be more than 105% of rents in similar apartments owned by the municipal housing company		
United Kingdom	No (rent caps apply for beneficiaries of Local Housing Allowance)	No	No, but review periods should be set in the lease

Source: Scanlon and Kochan 2011.

- Fully liberalizing only new rental units. Full liberalization in Spain (following the Boyer decree in 1984) resulted in "chaotic short-termism and high rents," so that soft control had to be reintroduced (Urban Tenancy Act 1994; World Bank, USAID, and TAPRII 2007).
- Permitting all rents to be raised within limits, such as by allowing the landlord to cover his operating costs including repairs.
- Further adjusting rents with quid pro quos: for example, permitting rent adjustments in exchange for investments financed by soft modernization loans as in the former German Democratic Republic.
- Limiting subrogation: In Spain, the 1984 decree abolished subrogation inter vivos but kept subrogation mortis causa (limited to two generations). In the Arab Republic of Egypt (box 3.1), a 1996 law freed the rental market for newly built and then-vacant units but grandfathered existing rent-controlled units for the duration of the contract (World Bank, USAID, and TAPRII 2007).
- Identifying and supporting needy tenants with housing allowances: In France, a housing allowance for families was created in 1948 by the same law that liberalized rents. This option is expensive for governments, but other solutions, such as limited decontrol, were found to have significant disadvantages (Malpezzi and Ball 1991).

Balance between Stability and Adaptability in Laws and Regulations

Reaching the right balance between the core legislation, which needs to be stable over time, and the rest of the rules, which need to be flexible and adaptable in specific economic situations such as periods of high inflation, is important. In countries with federal governments and those that have subnational

---

Box 3.1 Arab Republic of Egypt: Rent Decontrol in Midstream

Estimates from the 2006 census show that almost 32 percent (16.5 million units) of residential and other units in urban areas of Egypt were vacant or closed. The scale of urban vacancy, which was much more serious than in other emerging markets, is a specific and puzzling phenomenon of the Egyptian housing market. One explanation is that the sustained rapid appreciation in value over the past 30 years and the lack of alternative investment mechanisms until quite recently have led to a situation in which housing and real estate have consistently served as an inflation-proof savings and investment mechanism, without need of the rental yield.

Although this is the case in several emerging economies, including China, in Egypt the idea of owning rental housing was less attractive because of the imposition of rent control between 1944 and 1996. Rent control was coupled with stringent tenant protection laws, with the courts unwilling to evict tenants irrespective of noncompliance with contractual terms.

A decontrol law was passed in 1996. It freed the rental market for newly built and vacant units but grandfathered existing rent-controlled units for the duration of the contract. Since then, the rental market has been showing signs of dynamism. However, according to the TAPRII (Technical Assistance for Policy Reform II) Greater Cairo Housing Demand Survey of 2006, more than 40 percent of the housing stock was still locked under the rent control regime as a result of grandfathering. Moreover, the continued perception of uncertainty about the enforceability of the new rental law made many owners hesitant to put their unoccupied units to rent.

Because the rental market was unable to meet the growing needs of lower-income households, the only choice these households had was between units in new towns far from city centers and units in the informal sector. Estimates indicate that during the inter-census period (1996–2006) some 45 percent of new urban housing was created by the informal sector. Constrained by high standards for building and zoning, as well as a bureaucratic and costly permitting process, many small developers operate in the informal sector.

Source: World Bank, USAID, and TAPRII 2007.

---

legislatures, such as China, Germany, India, Mexico, and the United States, the same balance must be found between the need to harmonize with and the need to adapt to the local context. In many countries, the issue is not stability but the ability to change obsolete or ineffective laws. The difficulty arises because the rules that should be changed are typically embedded in the civil code.

Regular reviews of the rental sector should be conducted to see if changes in law have an effect. A government may do this, and the review also may be contracted to the private sector or to a university. These reviews should examine the size of the stock, the vacancy rate, investments and disinvestments, rent levels and their change, and types of rental contracts such as first rental, new contracts, renewed contracts, and current leases. These reviews should also focus on disputes and the average resolution time. The draft law of Morocco is a good example of how these recommendations have been adapted to the local context (box 3.2).

Box 3.2 Morocco: Revision of Legal Status of Rental

The share of rental housing in Morocco's urban housing stock decreased from 42 percent in 1982 to 29 percent in 2004. The rental stock is characterized by a high vacancy concentrated in apartment buildings, low profitability (estimated at 4.3 percent), and a negative leverage effect by credit. Ninety percent of the units belong to individuals. New investment is low, and most property investment consists of building or expanding their own house and renting a floor of it.

Landlord-tenant regulations favor the tenant, which results in contentious contractual relations, slow and complicated judicial procedures, and an inadequate capacity to enforce judicial decisions, particularly concerning eviction. No rent increase is allowed unless the landlord makes improvements.

A draft law has been prepared by the Ministry of Justice and the Ministry of Housing with support from the World Bank. The main features of the draft legislation are the following:

- A written lease is required, establishing clearly and explicitly the rights and obligations of the landlord and of the tenant
- The duration of the lease is specified in the written contract, if the parties so agree
- A description of the premises must be prepared when the lease is signed and when it expires
- The housing must be made habitable and decent
- Minor repairs are the responsibility of the tenant, not the landlord
- The tenant must not make improvements to the premises without the written agreement of the landlord
- The security to be provided by the tenant is increased from one to two months' rent
- The situations in which the owner may reoccupy the premises are precisely established
- The situations in which the lease may be cancelled are specified
- The rent is increased automatically every three years following the date of signature of the lease or the date of the last legal or regulated rent increase.

Revising the law is one of four requirements for the recovery of the rental sector. The next steps should consist of three actions:

- Making rental investments profitable, particularly investments in low-cost rentals
- Improving the ability of limited-income households to rent
- Professionalizing the leasing and management systems and processes.

Note: This information is based on a presentation by Mounia Diaa Lahlou, general director of real estate development of the Ministry of Housing of Morocco, at the fourth World Bank–IFC Global Housing Finance Conference in May 2010 in Washington, DC.

Tax Issues

Taxation is a tool that governments can use to encourage investment in rental housing. Real estate in general—and rental housing in particular—is often heavily taxed. It cannot be moved to another country as financial products can. Property taxes are one way that local governments raise the revenue they need to provide services for residents.

Owner-occupied main residences often receive benefits and tax subsidies that are superior to those of rental housing. This is one way in which governments encourage home ownership. Few countries are perfectly tenure neutral; the best example is Switzerland. In Switzerland, imputed rents, the estimated rental value of the unit, are treated like rental income.

Yet, while policies to provide more favorable treatment for home ownership than for rental are common, they often discourage ownership of rental properties. If the tax burden is too heavy, or is perceived as such, investors will find alternative ways of earning returns on capital. Individual or small owners might not have the option of funding alternatives. Instead, they can find ways to keep their properties out of the formal rental sector.

Comparing the rate of return between investments of different types is more difficult. That said, in many emerging countries, the choices offered to institutional investors are quite limited. They are even more limited for individuals.

There are several ways to assess the extent to which taxation of rental housing is an obstacle to investment. First, the effect of each tax on the rate of return can be measured. Although this might be difficult because of the different financial status of different owners, models can be developed for this measurement. Second, there are ways to estimate the effect of tax evasion. Studies performed in Mexico noted that the rate of income-tax evasion on rental units owned by individuals averaged 70–75 percent during 1998–2004. The fiscal cost to the government was estimated at 0.25 percent of gross domestic product (GDP) (ITAM 2006). Third, taxation of rental housing should be compared with taxation of alternative investment supports, financial products, and nonresidential real estate, as well as with owner-occupied residences.

When a benchmark exists, the usual rate of return is the 10- or 15-year government bond. The risk, liquidity, and capital gains of rental housing and bonds differ; however, lessons may be drawn from a simple comparison between the gross rates of return and the effect of taxation. Here is an example for Mexico in 2010 (for individual owners): The rate of return of the 10-year government bond was 7.5 percent. These bonds are tax-free for individuals. The gross rate of return on rental was estimated to be 7 percent in Mexico City and 10 percent elsewhere. Assuming that current expenses reduce this return by 25 percent and that the tax rate is 22.5 percent of gross income (30 percent of net income), the after-tax rate of return is 3.67 percent in Mexico City and 5.25 percent elsewhere.

In this case, it is easy to understand why investors do not deploy their capital toward rental housing and why individuals and small owners try to evade the system: the rate of return from rental housing is lower than the return on government bonds. When the risks of rental are factored in, this rate can actually be negative. Table 3.2 provides an international comparison of taxation of rental housing.

Table 3.2 Taxes on Private Rental Housing, Selected Countries

Phase	Purchase		Possession		Rental		Resale
Type of tax	VAT on new construction	Transaction tax	VAT on repairs	Property tax	VAT on rental income	Income or corporate tax	Capital gains tax
Denmark	No	Yes	Yes	Yes	No	Yes	Yes
France	Yes	Yes	Yes[a]	Yes	No	Yes	Yes
Germany	Yes	Yes[b]	Yes	Yes	No	Yes	Yes
Mexico	Yes	Yes	Yes	Yes	No	Yes	Yes
Netherlands	Yes	Yes	Yes	Yes	No	Yes[c]	Yes
United Kingdom	No	Yes	Yes	No	No	Yes	Yes
United States	n.a.[d]	Yes	n.a.[d]	Yes	n.a.[d]	Yes	Yes

Source: For Denmark, Germany, the Netherlands, the United Kingdom, and the United States, Oxley and Haffner 2010.
Note: n.a. = not applicable; VAT = value-added tax.
a. Reduced rate: 5.5 percent instead of 19.6 percent.
b. Including new construction.
c. Institutional investors are exempt from corporate tax.
d. No sales tax.

The taxation difference between owner-occupied housing and private rental housing can be affected by a number of other factors, such as:

- *Mortgage interest deduction:* This is quite widespread for landlords as either a business expense or an operating expense, yet varies from country to country for homeowners. In the United States, the mortgage interest deduction is applicable not only to the purchase of the main residence but also to other residential real estate, up to the maximum loan amount of US$1 million. This represents the largest housing subsidy for property ownership. Mortgage interest deductions also exist in Denmark and the Netherlands. They do not exist in Germany or anymore in the United Kingdom, except for low-income borrowers. France reintroduced the deduction in 2007 and then cancelled it again in 2011.

- *Depreciation allowance:* This is usually available to companies and is also available to individuals in a few countries. The annual rate is in the range of 2–2.5 percent in Australia, Germany, and Poland. It is higher in the United States. At 3.6 percent, this corresponds to 27.5 years. It is not applicable in France, Mexico, the Russian Federation, and the United Kingdom. Accelerated depreciation, where there is a higher rate during the first years, has been fundamental in Germany since World War II and was successfully used in France from 1996 to 2008.

- *Losses allowable against other income:* In Australia and Germany, there is no limit on the deduction of losses. The upper limit is US$25,000 in the United States and €10,700 in France. The fraction of deficit that exceeds the maximum may be carried forward for five years in France. It is not allowed in England.

- *Capital gains tax:* This is another tax for which owner-occupiers are usually granted preferential treatment: their main residence is exempt, often without limit. Preferential treatment is granted under certain conditions involving the duration of occupancy in Germany or the size of land area in Denmark. In the United States, the first US$250,000 of the gain is exempt from tax for individuals and the first US$500,000 for married couples. No gain is taxed if the gains are invested in a new property within two years. For rental and second homes, a heavy capital gains tax may help reduce speculation. However, it may also cause disinvestment and a sharper movement of properties into the informal, unregulated sector. A middle ground would be to significantly alleviate the capital gains tax after the first years, following the U.S. or French cases, to improve the total return for long-term investors. In general, to limit speculation, short-term gains are taxed more heavily than long-term gains. Australia and the United States apply the marginal rate of income tax if property is owned less than one year and a lesser rate thereafter. In 2012, France changed its flat tax rate to 34.5 percent for the first five years. The taxable base is reduced by 10 percent each year during the following 10 years, leading to a full exemption after 15 years. England offers no concession for long-term ownership (Oxley and Haffner 2010). Introducing a capital gains tax for owner-occupiers would be unpopular and could not be recommended.

- *Property taxes:* These are local taxes due from the owner. The amount taxed is usually based on the assessed value of the property or on its rental value, and tenure often has no effect. In a few cases, property taxes are biased in favor of ownership. In the United Kingdom, the "council tax" falls first on the tenant and only as a last resort on the owner (Oxley et al. 2010). In Morocco, the tax base for owner-occupiers is divided by four.

Tax Policy

In summary, tax codes are used to create or affect social and housing policies. For example, deductions and exemptions for mortgage interest expenses can have the effect of making home ownership more affordable, a goal that exists in most countries.

Tax policies, however, can also have unintended effects. A heavy tax burden might seem to be good social policy in rental housing for three reasons: the owner earns income, the property cannot be moved, and local governments need a base of revenue to provide services. However, a heavy burden can also cause a lack of investment in rental housing and push housing that could be registered and regulated into the informal sector instead. This can hurt tenants because in the informal sector they have less power and owners have less of an incentive to keep property in good condition.

Tax codes are complex. In evaluating their effect on rental property ownership, it is not just the overall rate that is relevant; the very specific elements that compose the details of the tax code are important as well. These elements include deductions, depreciation, capital gains, and other factors.

Financing: The Role of Credit

Financing, particularly long-term debt, plays a critical role in the success of a rental housing development. The lower the interest rate and the longer the amortization term, the lower the monthly debt service will be. Expenses will therefore be lower, net income will be higher, and the rate of return will be more favorable than on short-term, high-interest rate loans.

Credit plays a dual role: it reduces the amount of equity that is necessary, and, provided that the interest rate is less than the rate of return needed on invested capital, it leverages this equity.[2] The latter aspect is of primary importance for institutional investors: leveraging the equity is the only way to boost the rental return enough to allow rental housing to compete with alternative types of investment. Moreover, investors who are not speculators generally need long-term credit.

Financial Evaluation and Underwriting

Loans for rental housing are evaluated as loans to a project, not just as mortgages. This kind of underwriting is closer to commercial or project finance, because it relies heavily on examination of the cash flows generated by each project. As such, it is rarely subject to the automated loan approval procedures that have been used in single-family mortgage lending.

When a lending institution makes a decision to underwrite long-term debt for a rental project, it must do so in light of all the potential issues associated with long-term lending by banks in general. These issues include liquidity and interest-rate risks, instruments for matching asset and liability durations, existence of a demand for long-term paper, and the institution's overall corporate strategy.

A lender must also evaluate the business applying for the loan, including its management, its track record, the financial position of the owners or of the corporation, the market, the potential risks, and the competition. Evaluating the market is particularly critical because the lending institution must look at vacancy rates in the target market, local laws and regulations, and the overall economy in the areas served. It must assess potential developments that could affect the market, such as a factory closing, which would have a negative effect on the evaluation, or a new commercial and retail development, which would have a positive effect.

Unfortunately, long-term debt for rental housing is not available in most developing countries, although short-term loans may be available for construction or renovation. If there is no long-term debt, those considering building rental housing developments must provide much higher levels of equity. It is unlikely that an institutional investor would invest in multifamily rented buildings using only equity, unless the purchase price of the property is very low.

The lack of long-term debt also drastically reduces the capacity of individuals and small companies to invest in formal rental housing. When long-term debt for housing is not available, households that own a dwelling and wish to expand that property so that they can rent a room or purchase a unit for rental must do so with their own savings. A small- or medium-scale landlord might do so, but relying on cash raises the risk that the property will be kept in poor condition because there is little financial incentive to invest more capital for repairs and maintenance.

Market Lending for Rental Housing

In many countries, residential rental housing is perceived as less profitable and more risky than commercial rental. Thus, banks will tend to engage first in commercial, nonresidential lending. High-end residential rental may be an exception, especially in markets where little rental housing is available for professionals and executives. Moreover, unless the market is already developed, lenders will be reluctant to invest in the personnel, intellectual capital, and systems needed in this type of investment. Information on housing markets in general—and rental markets, in particular—is not always available, even in developed countries.

Lending to individual owners, who usually invest in only one unit at a time, is considered to be more risky than lending to owner-occupiers. This is because a landlord has a lesser stake in the property, which he can lose in a foreclosure without harming his own residence.

In the face of financial difficulty, owners or investors relinquish a property they do not occupy more easily than their own residence. Financial difficulties can arise for many reasons: a nonpaying tenant, declining market conditions, or natural disasters. Consequently, when a property is repossessed, much of the cost and delay of eviction is often passed to the lender.[3]

In most countries, there are few standardized debt instruments for multifamily mortgage debt and even fewer secondary market institutions that can purchase such debt. Sometimes financial products exist but require obtaining funds from multiple funding sources. The United States provides an interesting middle course: The Federal Housing Administration (FHA) will consider an owner-occupied property of up to four units as a single-family property for the purposes of providing mortgage insurance.

Financing Social Housing

Loans to finance full or partial social rental housing have specific features that have advantages and disadvantages for government and market players. They generally have longer loan terms than market conditions loans, often more than 30 years. This lengthened amortization period reduces the monthly debt burden. Sometimes there is government insurance or some type of credit enhancement. If subsidies are tied to the property, this, too, can strengthen the ability of a financial institution to underwrite the loan.

By contrast, such properties may also have high loan-to-value-ratios, which could increase the risk premium. Social and public properties are often located in less than desirable neighborhoods. Tenants' income sources are considered less steady than those in market-rate housing. Often, the quality of construction is not as high as it is in other types of rental properties.

To access government insurance or loan programs, owners of social housing usually must go through a more cumbersome application process and make commitments to serve certain groups or to keep the rents lower than market. In many countries, social housing and public housing are not operated as businesses. They are operated as costs in a governmental budget. Moreover, within larger public housing agencies, evaluating the performance of a particular property is difficult because it generally is included in a larger group of properties. Possibly, a well-performing property will subsidize a poor performer; but this situation also raises the risk that management may not spend in ways that benefit the properties and the residents. This risk makes underwriting a long-term loan challenging.

The United States is moving toward a different system, asset-based management. Here, management must demonstrate that a property or small group of properties can perform financially. If they do not, management is required to take steps to improve their performance, such as reducing vacancy rates. There are restrictions on how and how much the management of public housing authorities can take out of individual properties in exchange for management services.

If the property is not profitable and cannot be turned around, particularly if this situation is caused by poor conditions, the tenants can be given housing vouchers and the property can be rehabilitated, sold, or demolished after it goes through a governmental approval process. Private sector lending to public housing developments is very difficult. Pledging the assets of a public housing property in the United States requires direct approval from the secretary of the Department of Housing and Urban Development.

Capital Market Financing

Capital markets can be tapped through different avenues, such as the following:

- Bonds can be issued that are backed by mortgages originated by lending institutions.
- Direct financing of the rental project can be made through capital markets by bonds, with or without backing from a non-bank intermediary. This is used in the United Kingdom for the financing of social housing and in the United States with tax-exempt municipal bonds, issued in particular by bond-issuing authorities.
- Real estate investment trusts (REITs) are used in a few countries. In this mechanism, a security is sold to investors for the purpose of investing in real estate. REITs generally pledge high yields to investors. Moreover, they receive favorable tax considerations and are more liquid than investments made directly in a property.

Guarantees, Credit Enhancements, and Insurance Products

A number of financial products aim to make investment in residential rental housing more attractive. A distinction should be made between (a) insurance products devised to insure the rental income and (b) credit enhancement products for bonds that finance or purchase the mortgage loan or for bonds issued to finance the investment.

Among credit enhancement products, mortgage insurance is the most popular. Mortgage insurance protects lenders against loss on mortgage defaults. In so doing, it makes capital more readily available to developers. As one example of the countries examined, the U.S. Federal Housing Administration provides mortgage insurance for profit and nonprofit sponsors for the construction or rehabilitation of rental and cooperative housing for moderate-income groups (box 3.3).

Credit enhancement products ("bond wraps") provide security for bondholders and affect the bond rating. A higher rating translates into a more favorable pricing of the bonds and ultimately a lower mortgage rate. These products are distinct from mortgage insurance in that they typically do not look at the quality of individual credits within a pool. Rather, they provide additional security on top of what is already provided, such as by mortgage insurance.

In the United States, all bond-financed mortgages issued under tax-exempt, bond-financed programs must be credit enhanced, although the value of this enhancement declined after the mortgage crisis. There is another benefit. If a project meets the criteria for the low-income housing tax credit (LIHTC), it can receive a 4 percent credit, which is used to provide the developer with equity. Although this is lower than the normal credit, the developer does not have to compete to receive these credits, as the developer does in the case of the 9 percent credits. In Europe, local and central governments have often played a role in guaranteeing loans made to social housing institutions.

Box 3.3 United States: FHA's Multifamily Insurance Program

In this program, the U.S. Federal Housing Administration (FHA) provides insurance on multifamily mortgages that finance the construction, purchase, or rehabilitation of rental properties. These properties consist of five or more units because four or less are considered single-family properties. There are statutory mortgage limits that vary according to the location, the type of structure, and the size of the units.[a]

FHA multifamily insurance can go to either for-profit or not-for-profit owners or developers. The difference is that for-profit organizations may borrow only up to 90 percent of what the federal government terms "the HUD/FHA replacement cost" of the project, whereas nonprofit and governmental entities may borrow up to 100 percent.

One of the main advantages of this mortgage insurance is that it can be used on loans with amortization periods of up to 40 years. Funds for replacement reserves, repairs, and capital improvements may be included in the loans.

As of 2010, the FHA charged a 0.3 percent application fee and a 0.45 percent annual premium on the mortgage principal. The origination must go through an approved multifamily lender who reviews the transaction to ensure compliance with both FHA regulations and underwriting standards. An appraisal and market analysis is required.

a. See the HUD (Department of Housing and Urban Development) website,
http://nhl.gov/offices/hsg/mfh/progdesc/rentcoophsg221d3n4.cfm.

Enhancements for Social Housing Finance

Private markets do not always serve the financing needs for social housing. Governments will sometimes need to step in to address this market failure. Whereas some governments were once the main source of financing for social housing, public funding has not completely disappeared, but it has often changed shape.

France is the only country in the Eurozone in which the main funding source is, if not exactly public, at least centralized at the national level. (See country experience case for France and box 3.4 for a few other European cases.) In the United Kingdom, the 1988 Housing Act introduced private finance, moving associations to a mixed model of public grants and private bank loans. A direct

---

Box 3.4 Europe: Diversity of Social Housing Finance

In Europe, there is a broad range of mechanisms used to finance social housing.

In Germany, two systems coexist. The first includes an interest-free loan granted by the *Länder* (regions) through regional public banks. This loan can be granted to any investor, whether an individual or a company, for the construction of social rental housing. In return, the owner must sign an agreement on rent levels and eligibility criteria covering a period at least equal to the term of the loan, which is 30 years, on average. The second system consists of an operating subsidy granted during the term of the agreement.

The Netherlands has financial markets with long-term resources through pension funds. *Woningcorporaties* (housing companies) were organized to take advantage of these opportunities. The system includes social housing organizations, a mutual fund of solidarity—the CFV (Central Fund for Social Housing)—and a mutual guarantee fund—the WSW (Guarantee Fund for Social Housing) counter-guaranteed by the state. This system of three-tier security guarantees the solidarity and financial health of the sector, enabling it to benefit from favorable market rates. In Finland, the Public Housing Fund (ARA) does not distribute loans anymore. It enhances and guarantees loans made to organizations by financial institutions of various kinds that are competing to optimize the financing of operations.

Among the new member states, public funds remain in use, especially in Poland, Slovenia, and the Slovak Republic. They are subject to acute budgetary constraints. For example, in Poland, the public finance reforms of 2009 caused the liquidation of the National Housing Fund, which was operated by the public bank, BGK. Formally, the BGK is obliged to continue the programs developed by social housing associations (TBSs) with its own loans, but an overall review of the social rental housing program is under way.

In Slovenia, municipalities or companies under their control finance social housing service delivery for the lowest-income groups from their own resources. The Housing Fund of Slovenia offers favorable loans to nonprofit housing organizations, but municipal funds must contribute 40 percent. The Housing Fund can also act as co-investor or enter a public-private partnership.

In the Slovak Republic, social housing construction is financed from state budget resources as a combination of a subsidy (20–30 percent) and a soft loan from the State Housing Development Fund. The loan is for 30 years with a 1 percent interest rate.

---

subsidy covers 40–50 percent of the investment; private financing is necessary for the balance.

Guarantees are still offered to social housing projects by local governments in France and by mutual funds in the Netherlands and the United Kingdom.[4] In the Slovak Republic, the state guarantees loans for the construction of rental apartments for lower-income groups in order to provide incentives for the use of private finance. In the Netherlands, a complex system of guarantees for social housing loans has been put in place in which the state and municipalities play the role of last-resort guarantor on top of other guarantees.

In addition to public guarantees in Finland, the Netherlands, and the United Kingdom, providers in some countries have been implementing innovative ways of pooling risks. In England, there have been a number of club bond issues in which housing associations create a pool for joint bond issuance. In Switzerland, the Swiss Bond Issuing Cooperative raises funds for nonprofit housing entities that have formed a cooperative to reduce the cost of commercial loans. This system allows smaller nonprofit builders to join together, improving their access to private finance on more favorable terms.

Alternative or additional securities can be provided to the lender by securing reserve funds that can be tapped in the event of late payments or default. Recent loans to housing associations in the United Kingdom were secured by mortgages on social housing properties and cash reserves pledged to the issuer and bond trustee. In the event of default, the bond trustee will have the right to collect the rents and manage the secured property.

Subsidies

In every country, there is always a segment of the population that is poor and that would not be able to afford decent housing without some type of assistance. Even large, well-functioning rental sectors are not likely to provide units that are affordable for low-income households and mobile workers. For those who cannot afford market rents, various solutions should be considered, including tax incentives for private landlords, and subsidies and guarantees for specific "social landlords" such as private nonprofit companies and public-private partnerships.

Policy makers have a choice to make, although this choice is often constrained by budgetary forces. They may do nothing to assist lower-income populations, in which case they run the risk that some people will live in housing that is unaffordable, in poor condition, or unsafe, or that provides no tenure rights—or a combination of all these factors. Alternatively, they can provide housing directly, as in the case of public housing, or work within the market to provide some type of subsidy for those who cannot afford housing. They might also choose to do this for a targeted portion of the population.

Most experts believe that the percentage of a family's income dedicated to shelter should be no greater than 30–35 percent, or less for the lowest-income groups. In theory, to make a rental unit affordable for low-income households, the gap between the rent a tenant can afford and the market rent would need to be bridged. In the private sector, the market rent is the rent the landlord would be willing to accept in the absence of any additional compensation. In the case of public or social housing, the determination becomes more complicated. Often market rent is not a factor in the provision of rental housing. Instead, what is considered is the difference between the cost of housing and what a tenant pays.

Types of Subsidies

There are two ways to fill the gap between the affordable rent and market rent: one that brings the cost of housing down to an affordable level and one that provides financial support to the tenant to fill the gap between the market rent or its equivalent and the amount that a tenant can afford to pay. Sometimes the two are used in combination.

Supply-side subsidies are given to property owners and are intended to increase the supply of affordable housing. These subsidies can be through up-front grants, free or discounted land, or tax abatements. Their common purpose is to bring down the owner's costs so that a lower rent can be charged without reducing the owner's yield.

Demand-side subsidies, such as housing allowances or vouchers, are given to the tenant, the consumer of rental housing, or to the landlord on behalf of the tenant. The housing allowance is a regular payment aimed at increasing the rent a given household is able to pay.

Supply-Side Subsidies

Supply-side subsidies generally help with up-front costs and are targeted to certain segments of the population so they can have a direct effect on increasing the housing supply. A wide range of subsidies has been used over time in many countries and subsidies are often combined:

- Tax subsidies are used in many ways. In the European Union, this takes the form of a reduced value-added tax (VAT) rate. In the United Kingdom, it can be a full VAT exemption. Many local jurisdictions abate property taxes. French moderate rent housing (HLM) and several other European social housing companies benefit from income or corporate tax rebate or exemption. The LIHTC program in the United States uses a federally granted tax credit, which is awarded by each state on a competitive basis. This credit enables developers to raise equity for an affordable rental housing project (see box 3.5).
- Direct, low-interest public loans are provided in Austria through revolving provincial funds. Norway does the same through the Norwegian State Housing Bank. Other loans are subsidized through subsidies paid to lenders or use of off-market resources.
- Federal, state, regional, and local governments can provide direct grants. In the United States, states receive block grants that they sometimes use as

Box 3.5 United States: Low-Income Housing Tax Credit Program

The Low-Income Housing Tax Credit (LIHTC) uses the U.S. tax code as a way to raise equity for affordable housing developments. As a tax credit, it falls under the Department of the Treasury and does not appear in the Department of Housing and Urban Development's (HUD) budget. The program was created in 1986, following numerous attempts to stimulate affordable rental housing as part of broader tax reform legislation. The tax credit program was designed as a way for the federal government to stimulate the private and nonprofit sectors using the tax code instead of funding, building, and managing affordable housing projects. This is a blend of enabling the tools and financial abilities of the private sector with establishing a targeted system to carry out the policy of increasing affordable housing.

Operation

Although the LIHTC is a federal program and Congress set forth the basic criteria, each state creates policies to award those tax credits over and above the federal minimum standards. States also manage the day-to-day operations of the program, generally through state housing finance agencies (HFAs).

HFAs exist in all states and in some municipalities. Some are limited in purpose and serve only as a bridge to the private sector, such as through tax incentives and bond issuance. Others are more full-service entities whose programs include managing federal and state grant programs, housing trust funds, funding for housing development, down-payment assistance to homebuyers, and rental assistance to low-income families.

Each state receives an allocation of credits from the federal government, based on its population. The HFA then develops a "qualified allocation plan" that creates the policies governing the awards, which are highly competitive.

To be eligible for this program, federal law requires a developer to make a commitment to keep the development affordable for a minimum of 15 years. This means caps on income and rent based on the particular geographic area. Developers submit applications to the state's allocating agency. If a development is awarded an allocation of credits, the developer receives a tax credit of 9 percent of the qualified costs for each of the next 10 years. In general, the costs associated with this basis are most of the costs incurred for the project, except for land and the costs of raising capital.

Because the developer needs the capital in the near term to construct the property, he sells the credit to an investor or tax credit syndicator. The amount that the developer receives depends on the market value at the time. In the early years of the program, investors were paying only 45 percent of the 10-year value of the credit.

Results

As the program matured, investors came to believe that it was a very safe investment, and they were willing to accept lower rates of return. As a consequence, the value of the credits increased. By the peak of the market in 2006, the percentage of the 10-year credit that the developers were receiving had more than doubled, to more than 90 percent. In the wake of the mortgage crisis, the equity percentage dropped to approximately 65 percent and has moved upward since then. Much of the reason for the drop was that the largest purchasers of the credits were

box continues next page

Box 3.5 United States: Low-Income Housing Tax Credit Program *(continued)*

Fannie Mae and Freddie Mac. After these entities were taken over by the government, they no longer purchased tax credits. Other investors subsequently moved into the market.

Even with this layer of equity, a project sometimes does not provide positive cash flow because of the reduced rents. To fill the financial gap, developers seek other sources, such as federal funds, foundation grants, and soft second mortgages.

As more developers saw the benefits of the tax credits, more applied and the program became extremely competitive. In some states, demand exceeded supply by more than 10 to 1. This enabled those who allocated the credit to give greater consideration to developers who were willing to commit to even lower-income people, who would keep the housing affordable for a longer period, who would provide social services to the tenants, and who would build in areas determined to be in need of affordable rental housing.

Since it was created, the LIHTC program has helped to create more affordable rental housing in the United States than any other program. It has created a financial system that has been sustained for more than two decades. This type of financing mechanism is quite different from one in which the government finances, builds, and manages the housing. It enables the discipline of the private financial sector and the private housing management sector to be used in affordable housing, adding both strength and depth.

The housing that is built under the program is often indistinguishable from privately owned, market-rate housing. The developments generally blend into the community in which they are located. However, the program cannot work in every situation and cannot address all affordable housing needs. A country evaluating this program must have a tax system that is vibrant enough to create a tax credit program and companies with a tax burden deep enough to use this type of tax offset.

Evaluation

There are some criticisms of the program. First, because of the rents that must be charged, it serves residents on the higher end of the low- to moderate-income scale. Those who have very low incomes cannot afford these units without a much deeper form of subsidy. In many properties, housing vouchers are used to provide subsidies for the tax credit unit, combining supply-side credits in the form of equity from the credits and demand-side subsidies in the form of housing vouchers.

Second, some argue that, in some communities, the difference between market rents and the social rents established in the program is not wide enough to justify the loss to the federal treasury through this incentive.

Third, because of state priorities targeting lower-income communities, it is not uncommon to see certain geographic areas overbuilt, with supply exceeding demand. At the same time, affordable housing needs in higher-income areas go unmet, even if there are low-income families in those areas that need such housing.

Fourth, the financial elements of the program can be subject to the vicissitudes of the financial market. Although the program saw a steady increase in the value of equity, the years after the mortgage crisis yielded much lower percentages of equity. This change makes it difficult for developers who invested capital planning on equity at the higher price to adjust to such a deep drop. The effect is worsened when developers also see more difficulty in accessing

box continues next page

Box 3.5 United States: Low-Income Housing Tax Credit Program *(continued)*

the debt markets. This last factor should also guide those who seek to develop such program and will note how important the tax code and financial markets of a particular country are in evaluating if and how the program can work.

Note: The technical definition of affordability is either (a) at least 20 percent or more of the residential units in the development are both rent restricted and occupied by individuals whose income is 50 percent or less of the area median gross income, or (b) at least 40 percent or more of the residential units in the development are both rent restricted and occupied by individuals whose income is 60 percent or less of the area median gross income. Under either standard, low-income tenants can be charged a maximum monthly rent of 30 percent of the maximum eligible income.

supply-side subsidies. In France, the use of part of the main (regulated) savings products, which is liquid and offers a tax-exempt return, to fund extremely long-term loans to social housing development at below-market conditions is a form of implicit subsidy.

• Municipalities may provide land for social housing programs, through sale or long-term lease for free or at a low price.
• State and local governments may provide funding for necessary infrastructure improvements.
• Governments may provide investors with guarantees for their loans.

In many cases, several types of subsidies are used simultaneously.

• In Scotland and in England, there is a large up-front subsidy. This amount is in addition to the benefit of the full VAT exemption, so that the loan, which is a market loan, is relatively small. In France, the up-front budget subsidy has decreased over time and the amount of the loan, which is soft and off-market, has increased.
• In the United States, the HOPE VI (Housing Opportunities for People Everywhere) program provides grants to developers in exchange for broad community developments, which almost always include both publicly and privately owned subsidized rental housing. To make the project work, developers use additional types of subsidies, such as tax credit equity, foundation grants, federal block-grant money, and low-interest loans.

Evaluation

Sometimes supply-side subsidies are provided before or during the early stages of construction, and sometimes they entail longer-term commitments. Examples of longer-term commitments include interest rate subsidies and guarantees for the term of the loan and tax benefits, such as exemption from property taxes, that can last 25 years in France. Estimating the cost of supply-side subsidies can be difficult, especially if the economic environment changes after the subsidies are put in place. Interest-rate subsidies, however, are difficult to measure, are not transparent, and put the government at risk in an inflationary environment.

Although supply-side subsidies are generally used on the front end of a construction or rehabilitation process and are easier to calculate, they too pose challenges. There is often no effective mechanism for ensuring that the property is properly maintained. In addition, targeting supply-side subsidies is difficult. To make a project work, supply-side subsidies distinguish only a small number of categories, such as lower-income persons, those who are elderly or disabled, or evacuees from disasters.

The benefits of a subsidy are sometimes hard to measure. For example, unless there is a direct tradeoff between the costs of the subsidy and the benefit to the tenant, it is difficult to know how much of the reduction in a capital cost is passed on to the tenant. Some governments put caps on the cost of construction or rehabilitation. This must be done carefully. If the caps are either too high or nonexistent, then wasteful spending can ensue. If they are too low, then the housing will be of poor quality.

Governments sometimes budget the full or a significant portion of the potential cost of a mortgage default guarantee. This reduces the attractiveness of a subsidy even if there is no immediate budgetary cost. In a default on an insured property, not only does the claim have to be paid, but the insurer will take possession of the property as well. If the property has fallen into disrepair, its market value will have declined and the insurer will have to sell the property at a loss or expend funds for capital improvements. In the case of government insurance, the insurer may have to pay tenant relocation costs if the property houses low-income tenants who receive rental subsidies and becomes uninhabitable.

Governments sometimes prompt owners to sell part of their amortized stock to current tenants. These sales were done on a large scale in the United Kingdom. They remain mostly on a marginal scale in other countries. Landlords rarely favor such sales because they are reluctant to part with their best units or their best tenants. Those whose stock is composed mainly of apartment buildings face additional challenges, including the management of condominiums.

Special Types of Subsidies

Other types of subsidies involve tenants, employers, and social organizations. The subsidies are usually provided in exchange for partial ownership or for a long-term reduction in the tenant's rent. For example:

- In France, a mandatory contribution for all private nonagricultural enterprises with at least 20 employees was introduced in 1953, with a rate initially set at 1 percent of payroll, hence the common name of "Housing 1 Percent." It is a revolving fund. Loan repayments are recycled into new loans. The traditional use of the Housing 1 Percent in the social rental sector is for subsidies and low-interest loans for the construction and improvement of housing units. In return, all or a portion of the units in the social rental housing stock are reserved for the employees of contributing firms.

- In Austria, tenants whose share is more than €50 per square meter get a right to purchase after 10 years of occupation. In Denmark a deposit of 2 percent of the cost of housing, refundable upon departure, is required. Households can get a loan from the municipality to finance the deposit.

Figure 3.2 Poland: Finance Plan for TBS Programs

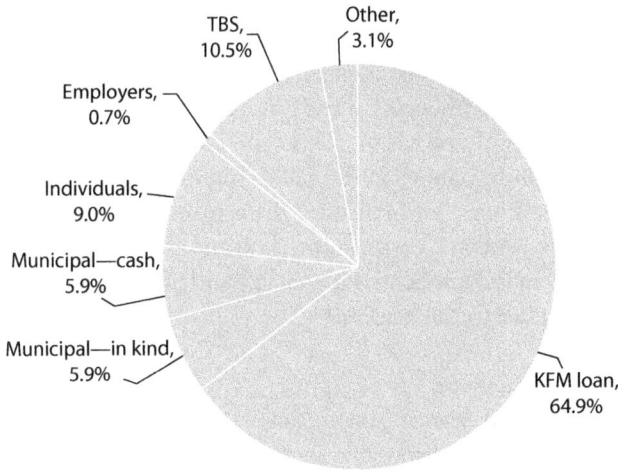

Source: Poland, Ministry of Infrastructure, investor survey 2008.
Note: KFM is the National Housing Fund; TBS is the Society for Social Housing.

- Other funds come from a growing trend toward diversification of the activities of social housing agencies in the lucrative commercial activities that are cross-subsidies for social housing. For example, this is the case of social housing associations (TBSs) in Poland, *woningcorporaties* in the Netherlands, and housing associations in the United Kingdom.

- In Poland, some employers support TBSs, but only for a very small share. TBSs also require tenants to fill part of the gap between the cost of construction and the amount of the public loan, which has a maximum loan-to-value ratio of 70 percent. This participation is refunded when tenants leave, indexed on the regional construction cost index, but gives them no right to purchase. See figure 3.2.

Demand-Side Subsidies

Demand-side subsidies give direct financial benefits to tenants or to others on behalf of the tenants. They provide ongoing support to ensure that the housing is affordable. These types of subsidies include allowances, vouchers, direct payments, and hybrids:

- Housing allowances in the form of direct payments to the tenants to assist them with monthly payments are given in most European countries.
- Vouchers are given to tenants so that they can find rental housing. The tenant selects the dwelling, and the landlord receives the difference between a portion of the tenant's income and a predetermined rent. Sometimes this is done on the basis of a formula; other times the amount of assistance is determined by an assessment of area market rents.

- Project-based rental subsidies are sometimes given directly to landlords of eligible units. They must select tenants who meet certain income criteria. The rent is set according to guidelines similar to those for housing vouchers, and tenants pay a similar portion of their income. Project-based subsidies make it easier for owners to get financing if the government makes a long-term commitment for the subsidy provision. This type of subsidy was the most common form in the United States in the 1970s but now plays only a small role.
- In Belgium, Luxembourg, and Portugal, the rent in the social housing sector is first calculated based on a cost-rent method and then adapted to household income. This system is complicated to manage and often requires the payment of balancing subsidies to the landlord.

Scales of Housing Allowances

The scales of housing allowance aim to keep the rent burden at or below a proportion of a household's disposable income that makes it possible to meet other household expenses, generally in the range of 30–35 percent.

In France, the amount of the allowance is based on a calculation of the part of the housing expense to be paid by a household. A "rate of participation" is applied to the household's resources. This rate varies according to income, location, and family size. The amount of the subsidy is then simply deducted: it is equal to the difference between the eligible expense (the rent up to a maximum level plus a lump sum for utilities) and the household's participation.

The German *Wohngeld* works partly on the same principle. The scale takes into account family composition, housing characteristics, and location (in six areas since 1991). It is intended to maintain the payment-to-income ratio including utilities in the range of 15–35 percent, depending on household size.

In the United States, there are two systems of direct rental assistance: tenant based and project based. Tenant-based rental assistance gives residents a voucher that pays the difference between the "fair market rent" and 30 percent of the tenants' incomes. The tenant can change residences and keep the subsidy. In project-based rental assistance, the federal subsidy is tied to the unit itself and not to the tenant. Residents of public housing make rental payments under this same formula.

In the United Kingdom, housing benefits exist in both the public and the private sector. The aid covers the entire rent but excludes most expenses for households whose income is below a governmentally determined level called "Income Support." Until 1995, the rent determination was what the rent officer considered reasonable. Since 1996, the rent must be less than a local area reference rent corresponding to the average after excluding high and low outliers.

After a tenant's income goes above Income Support, assistance was reduced by €65 for every €100 increase in income. Some considered this a "poverty trap" because the overall marginal tax rate, taking into account personal assistance, exceeded 90 percent. To overcome the first effect, the housing benefit was partially reformed in 2008. The Local Housing Allowance replaced it for private tenants; its entitlement is determined by rules about the size and composition of the household and local rent levels. There are upper limits to what can be paid.

The proportion of beneficiaries in the population and the average aid granted vary considerably from one country to another. In Germany, the beneficiaries of *Wohngeld* represent 2 percent of households since the separation of special aid in 2005, whereas it was 9 percent under the previous system. France's beneficiaries are 23 percent of the population, a share more than 11 times higher than Germany's. France and the United Kingdom have, respectively, the highest proportion of beneficiaries and the highest amount of average aid. Overall, in 2010, the fiscal cost of housing allowances accounted for 0.05 percent of GDP in Germany, 0.18 percent in the United States, 0.82 percent in France, and 1.44 percent in the United Kingdom.[5]

Evaluation

Housing allowances can be extremely expensive. In France and the United Kingdom, housing allowances constitute the vast majority of the budget dedicated to housing by the nation. In the United States, they constitute the largest portion of the budget of HUD, the key federal housing agency.

Because demand-side subsidies are expensive, they often cannot serve the need in a particular market. In the United States, the demand for Housing Choice Vouchers, also known as Section 8 vouchers, is so high in certain cities that the waiting lists are closed. In theory, housing vouchers leave more freedom for households to choose the type, location, and cost of their dwellings and to change units. However, this assumes that tenants can find an apartment for rent that accepts these vouchers, which is not always the case.

If demand-side subsidies are given only for a limited period of time, there is the risk of dislocating tenants when the subsidy expires, if they cannot afford the market rent. By contrast, an increase in income sometimes leads to an increase in rent or a deduction or elimination of subsidies. This can occur when a tenant must certify income periodically, generally each year. It can also result in the loss of right to maintain occupancy, although this is less common. If the subsidy is tied to a particular unit, there is generally some period of time in which to secure another apartment. A fall in income might lead to a reduction in rent, although this can be done only if the tenant can demonstrate that his or her income has declined.

An economic downturn can increase the number of beneficiaries. It may also increase the average amount of a subsidy, because subsidies are usually based on some type of scale. This is the case in Europe. The result is higher cost and budget pressure. However, demand-side subsidies may be seen as a Keynesian type of stimulus during times of economic downturn, which adds to the social impact of an allowance. In a budgetary crisis, subsidies may be reduced to save costs, especially if government funds are cut overall. The risk is that an attempt to contain the fiscal cost may cause significant social problems by reducing tenants' solvency and access to decent housing.

Demand-side subsidies are sometimes seen to have an inflationary effect on rents in the private sector. This was the case in France when the government extended assistance to students (Laferrère and Le Blanc 2004). In the social sector too, landlords may be tempted to increase rents more strongly in programs in which rents are better covered by allowances.

If an increase in aid too generously compensates a decrease in income because of job loss, it might discourage the resumption of employment. Some have considered this to be a poverty trap: tenants might give up all or most of their future income gains so as not to lose their present benefits, as in the case of the housing benefit in the United Kingdom.

Notes

1. Similarly, in the United Kingdom, Peter Rachman gave his name to "Rachmanism," now a synonym for exploitation of tenants. In France, the fictional Mr. Vautour's name does not need to be translated; in this case, the vulturous landlord character of the mid-19th century was created for theater on the basis of the name.

2. An alternative solution is to buy shares of real estate investment trusts (REITs) instead, as mentioned earlier.

3. The opposite may be seen: in repossessions for owner default, even a tenant who has been regularly paying his rent may be evicted. This is the case in some parts of the United States when rental housing owners do not honor their financial obligations.

4. In return, 20 percent of the units financed with the guaranteed loan are reserved.

5. Author's calculations using data from Eurostat, http://www.statistics.gov.uk (annual abstract, table 19.3); Destatis (*Wohngeld tabellen*) (Germany); "Compte du logement 2012:101" (France); U.S. Bureau of Economic Analysis and HUD.

References

Casa-Arce, Pablo and Albert Saiz. 2007. "Do Courts Matter? Rental Markets and the Law." Working Paper, Universitat Pompeu Fabra, Barcelona.

ITAM (Instituto Tecnológico Autónomo de México). 2006. "Medición de la evasión fiscal en México." ITAM, Mexico City.

Kemp, Peter A. 2007. *Housing Allowances in a Comparative Perspective*. Bristol, U.K.: The Polity Press.

———. 2008. Workshop for the 2008 ENHR (European Network for Housing Research) Conference, Dublin, July 6–9.

Laferrère, Anne, and David Le Blanc. 2004. "How Do Housing Allowances Affect Rents? An Empirical Analysis of the French Case." *Journal of Housing Economics* 13 (1): 36–67.

Malpezzi, Stephen, and Gwendolyn Ball. 1991. *Rent Control in Developing Countries*. Washington, DC: World Bank.

Oxley, Michael, and Marietta Haffner. 2010. "Housing Taxation and Subsidies: International Comparisons and the Options for Reform." Joseph Rowntree Foundation, York, U.K.

Oxley, Michael, Ros Lishman, Tim Brown, Michael Haffner, and Joris Hoekstra. 2010. *Promoting Investment in Private Rented Housing Supply: International Policy Comparisons*. London: Department for Communities and Local Government.

Poland, Ministry of Infrastructure. 2008. Investor survey. Warsaw.

The Spanish Urban Tenancy Act 1994 (Ley de Arrendamientos Urbanos).

Scanlon, Kath, and Ben Kochan. 2011. "Toward a Sustainable Private Rented Sector. The Lessons from other Countries." LSE, London.

World Bank, USAID (U.S. Agency for International Development), and TAPR (Technical Assistance for Policy Reform) II. 2007. "A Road Map for Housing Policy Reform in Egypt: Developing a Well-Functioning Housing System and Strengthening the National Housing Program." Washington, DC, and Cairo.

CHAPTER 4

Recommendations and Conclusion

Abstract

The recent financial crisis demonstrated that not everyone wants to or can afford to purchase a home. Yet there is still a bias against rental housing. By taking a systematic approach to housing and by including rental housing as an important part of the system, policy makers can ensure a balanced approach that can support future growth.

Introduction

UN-HABITAT (United Nations Human Settlements Programme) noted that "Governments should not close their eyes to reality. They should not perpetuate the myth of the achievability of universal home ownership. Instead, they should accept that millions of households live in rental housing and that at some point in their lives most people need rental accommodation" (UN-HABITAT 2003, 3). Few listened to this advice in 2003, but the mortgage crisis has shed light on the need for alternatives to home ownership.

Each country now needs to look at multiple factors to determine whether it should engage in the rental market, how it should engage, and whom it should serve. One factor, of course, is family income. Another is the condition in which people live and whether they are in safe dwellings, regardless of whether they own or rent. One of the main decision points is what people the country wants to assist.

Does it want to:

- Help people who are living in slums or poor-quality housing or who are living along the banks of waterways and are in danger of being flooded?
- Use its resources in collaboration with employers to house factory or service workers?
- Assist the poor, the elderly, or the disabled?

In some cases, governments have even chosen to help develop higher-income people in rental markets, although that has generally been part of a broader economic development strategy.

The most important recommendation is for governments to acknowledge that rental housing is an important component of the housing system. With that acknowledgment, many barriers can begin to be reduced, and the positive elements added. If a national housing policy exists or is under development, this is an excellent document in which to add a section on rental housing, subsidies, and finance.

Assessment of the Rental Sector

The next priority is for governments to develop sufficient knowledge by performing an assessment of the rental sector, preferably in the context of an overall market assessment. This type of study could help guide the specific details of a national housing policy and of ways to intervene in market development.

This assessment should include the following aspects:

- Compare household characteristics (age, occupation, income, family type, and size) and housing conditions (location, type of building, size, and equipment of the unit)
- Discover tenants' reasons for renting and the type of landlord, such as an individual, real estate company, institution, public, nonprofit, or nongovernmental organization
- Evaluate the balance between supply and demand
- Monitor variations in market rent levels
- Evaluate conflicts and the conflict resolution process
- Compare the costs of renting and owning, including obstacles to access to credit
- Compare rental return and risk with alternative investments by market segment.

The main data for a basic assessment are available from population census and housing surveys. Adding a few questions for tenants in housing or consumption surveys and gathering market information from real estate agents will be useful. Courts in the major cities should be able to provide data on conflicts.

Legal and Contractual Framework

An analysis of the legal framework is also quite important. If the legal system is perceived to be unfair to landlords, then they will not invest in rental housing or will keep the housing informal. If it is perceived to be unfair to tenants, then they are likely living in housing that is in poor condition and where they do not have security of tenure. This will then raise issues that a government must face.

Actions governments take in the legal and regulatory sector should create systems that encourage rental properties that are safe and habitable. Governments need to ensure that the rights of landlords and tenants are balanced and that laws and processes that deal with eviction are fair to both parties, efficient, and transparent. Much of this will have to be done on the state and local levels, although guidance can be given from national governments.

Encouraging the development of standardized contracts will be beneficial. There should be a list of documents that is part of a rental file. The main items to be included here are (a) the definition and description of the rental unit, (b) the duration and termination of contracts, (c) rent setting and rent increases, (d) procedures for resolving conflicts and stability, and (e) adaptability of legal dispositions.

A rental contract should specify a fixed period for the rental. The length of this period should be neither too short, in order to give the tenant stability, nor too long, in order to give the landlord some flexibility. It should cover the key issues that are necessary to have a strong, two-party agreement.

The system should codify the differences between various forms of rental housing:

- Between the units that are the main residence of a household, to which higher protection should by granted, and other rental accommodation such as vacation homes
- Between housing for one person or a family and housing that is shared
- Between social housing and other rentals.

The right balance is required between the core legislation, which needs to be stable over time, and the rest of the rules, which need to be flexible. Main regulations should be consolidated in a single law, not scattered in several texts, including the civil code. In federal countries and those that have subnational legislatures, a similar balance should be sought between the need to harmonize and the need to adapt to the local context.

Rent Control and Rent Setting

Rent setting and rent increases are key issues. Areas that have had strong rent control systems instituted these regulations to protect tenants. However, over time, it became clear that rent control inhibited development and that there were better ways to provide affordable housing that was clearly targeted to particular beneficiaries.

In a permanent system, distinction should be made between four cases:

- New rental units created through construction or conversion: rent should be freely negotiated, rules may be set to avoid "usury rents"
- Units that become vacant for various reasons: in most, rent restrictions should be lifted, although there may be some limits using "reference" or "reasonable" rents

- Renewed leases to existing tenants: indexation can be used in addition to the free rent and the reference-linked rent
- Indexation to an official index or no increase in a lease if it is a short lease of up to one year in duration.

The decisions concerning one of these issues interact with others. For example, where it is difficult to increase the rent after its initial setting, landlords will try to set the initial rent at the highest possible level.

If a country, or a city or region within a country, has a rent control system, this will likely harm the possibility of rental housing development. If the government chooses to move away from such a system, it must be done carefully, as was done in the Czech Republic.

Conflict Resolution

There are countries where the legal process is cumbersome and others where it is far more straightforward.

In order to avoid lengthy and costly legal procedures in the former case, conflict settlement between landlords and tenants should be made easier by the introduction of non judicial remedies, such as mediation and arbitration. Mediation aims to end the dispute prior to any legal action by entering into a reconciliation process led by a third party who is trained and who is supposed to be neutral in the dispute. Arbitration is intended to settle the dispute by an arbitral tribunal, an arbitrator or a panel of arbitrators.

Sometimes these are considered phases one and two in dispute resolution, with the parties agreeing to try mediation first. If the parties do not agree, the process can move to arbitration unless the arbitration is binding. Sometimes judicial appeals are permitted, other times they are not.

Such alternatives to the judicial process were introduced in Morocco in 2005 with a mandate that covers all disputes between private parties. In France, "Commissions Départementales de Conciliation" are intended to settle rental disputes both in the private and public housing sectors, thus avoiding going to court. In the United States, certain jurisdictions, such as Boston, Massachusetts, have specialized housing courts. Another specialized entity is Regie du logement in the Canadian province of Quebec (box 4.1). These examples are movements to conflict resolution that are quick, fair, and responsive to local circumstances.

Ensuring that property laws and regulations that are fair, open, and transparent and that give both tenant an owner clearly defined processes and timelines for resolution will only go part of the way toward allaying owners' and tenants' concerns.

Tax Issues

The tax system is similar. If the tax burden is too high and if it brings down the rate of return so that, on a risk-adjusted basis, the rate of return is lower than safer investments, then large-scale investments will not be made.

Box 4.1 Quebec (Canada): The Regie du logement[a]

The Regie du logement is a specialized tribunal that has competence in residential lease matters. Its mission consists of deciding the applications that have been submitted within the framework of simple rules of procedure that respect natural justice. It also informs both parties of their rights and obligations related to the lease to avoid conflicts that occur due to the ignorance of the law. It also promotes reconciliation between landlords and tenants.

The Regie also keeps a watch, in certain circumstances, on the conservation of the housing stock and, in those cases, makes sure that the rights of the tenants are protected.

The Regie du logement decides in first instance, to the exclusion of any tribunal:

- On any application concerning the lease of a dwelling where the sum claimed, the value of the thing claimed, or of the interest of the applicant in the object of the application is less than $70,000
- On any application, whatever the amount, concerning a lease renewal, rent fixing, a repossession, a division of the dwelling, a change of destination or a substantial enlargement of the dwelling or the lease of a dwelling in low-rental housing.

The Regie du logement also decides on any application pertaining to the conservation of dwellings and the protection of tenants:

- Demolition of a unit where there is no municipal regulation that provides for it
- Sale of a rental building within a building complex
- Conversion of residential buildings to divided co-ownership or cooperatives.

The jurisdiction of the Regie du logement governs:

- Leases relating to the services, accessories, and dependencies of a dwelling
- The lease of a mobile home placed on a chassis or on land where a mobile home is placed
- The lease of a room, except if situated in a health or social services institution (except pursuant to article 1974 of the civil code of Quebec), in a hotel establishment or if not more than two rooms are rented or offered for rent in the principal residence of the landlord and if the room has neither a separate entrance from the outside nor sanitary facilities separate from those used by the landlord.

However, the jurisdiction of the Regie does not cover the lease of a dwelling leased as a vacation resort or the lease of a dwelling in which over one-third of the total floor area is used for purposes other than residential.

The Regie can also revise its own decisions concerning an application where the sole object is the fixing or the revision of the rent.

Other decisions rendered by the Regie can be appealed with the permission of a judge of the Court of Quebec, with the exception of:

- The recovery of a debt not exceeding $7,000
- An authorization to deposit rent
- An application concerning the conservation of dwellings.

a. See http://www.rdl.gouv.qc.ca.

Smaller scale investments could be made, but they too are likely to be in the informal sector.

From a tax perspective, investment in rental housing needs to be on an even playing field with similar investments. The tax code should ensure that rental real estate does not carry a higher tax burden than other real estate in such elements as allowable deductions and depreciation periods. This will help to ensure that the return, the risk, and the liquidity of the housing investment are comparable. These financial prerequisites should help investors get better access to market finance.

If a country wants to develop or strengthen its rental housing sector, it needs to create a balanced tax framework in line with international practices, using as models the countries that have a large private rental sector, such as the Federal Republic of Germany, Switzerland, and the United States. National and regional differences should be considered as well, since what works in these Western countries may not work in all countries.

A good tax model should include:

• Deductibility of main costs such as maintenance work and interest paid
• Economic depreciation
• Possibility of using losses to offset taxes on other types of income.

Additional measures could be taken temporarily by governments willing to give a strong push to investment in rental housing. This has been the case in the Federal Republic of Germany and France. Other measures could also be introduced to ensure commitments to provide affordable rental.

A government designing a housing policy to move properties from the informal sector to the regulated sector must be careful that its initial effort is not punitive. It could consider providing temporary tax exemptions to properties currently in the informal sector and incentives to put the properties into safe, habitable condition. It might also consider financial incentives for property improvement.

Governments might see what can be done to encourage the development or strengthening of insurance markets for both owners and tenants. Some of the necessary adjustments should be made through taxation and insurance products.

Finance

Long-term capital is essential in developing a large-scale real estate market. Long-term capital is also helpful to individual owners who would like to purchase or renovate other units. Identifying and establishing ways to stimulate equity for rental properties can be important in filling any financial gap. Rarely does a banking system or a government provide equity capital or long-term debt for investment in multifamily residential rental developments. Even when financing is available, some type of additional subsidy, such as a grant or a tax incentive, is usually needed to reduce the amount of debt and provide investors with an adequate rate of return.

Whereas many countries do not have financial systems that could provide construction and long-term financing, governments could step in with assistance or with supply-side subsidies. These could include:

- Bonds issued for multifamily development, as is done in the United States.
- A housing development fund, which would make financing available to developers. Although real estate investment trusts might be possible, there are not many countries where the tax structure could make them feasible.
- Stimulation of a rental income guarantee or insurance scheme where a portion of the rental income is paid in the event of nonpayment by the tenant. This exists in the United Kingdom, as an example. However, the government must be careful that all of the burden does not fall on it, and that there are strict and transparent insurance standards to avoid moral hazards.
- Grants, land, or infrastructure provided free or at a reduced cost in exchange for keeping rents affordable for certain income populations.

Subsidies

There are two ways to fill the gap between the affordable rent and market rent: supply-side subsidies, which bring the cost of housing down to an affordable level, and demand-side subsidies, which provide direct financial support to the tenant.

Supply-Side Subsidies

For supply-side subsidies, questions include whether to subsidize only the cost of construction of housing or to subsidize recurrent costs such as building management and maintenance as well. Up-front subsidies such as grants have an immediate budget impact, whereas tax incentives can be used over a long period. Supply-side subsidies should take into account the data available when tenants began renting, although accurate information can be difficult to obtain.

Direct up-front subsidies from the federal or national and regional or local governments are probably the simplest and most transparent ones. They also do not create long-term commitments as loan guarantees do, and they reduce the amount of the loan, which is reassuring to the lender. Unfortunately, because of the fiscal situation in many countries and cities, there is pressure to reduce this type of subsidy.

Because supply-side subsidies represent a financial commitment from the government to the owner, governments should obtain social commitments in exchange for their contribution. This generally means income limits on those served combined with lower-than-market rents for an agreed-on period of time. Governments should look at the value of the subsidy in relation to the cost of the social benefits that are achieved. In addition, consideration should be given to what happens after the commitment period expires.

Demand-Side Subsidies

Demand-side subsidies should be designed so that they are transparent, efficient, fair, and clearly targeted to specific populations. One of the main ways this can be done is through a housing allowance or a voucher. These are common in several Western European countries.

Demand-side subsidies, housing allowances or vouchers, are the most effective way to make rental housing affordable to low-income households. Yet they entail heavy fiscal commitments and require the collection and update of information on beneficiaries. Because demand-side subsidies have less effect on housing supply than supply-side subsidies, both should be used in parallel whenever housing needs remain important.

The amount of direct assistance to low-income tenants should be linked to household income, to the rent, and to the type of household or the family size. The subsidy should be adjusted accordingly, as quickly as possible, especially to compensate for major losses of income, such as death, illness, or unemployment.

The scales should be carefully designed so as to avoid the creation of poverty traps, inflationary effects, and a lack of incentive to adjust the size of the unit to the real needs of households. The scales should be simple and transparent so that beneficiaries understand how they are calculated.

Combining Supply- and Demand-Side Subsidies

In general, serving the lowest-income groups through supply-side mechanisms only is difficult, if not impossible. Additional subsidies will be needed, such as vouchers, housing allowances, subsidies paid to the landlord, or ongoing payments for maintenance, management, and capital improvements.

Housing allowances and supply-side subsidies can be used in parallel, especially in countries where housing needs remain important. Local or national governments that consider introducing housing allowances should also be aware of the heavy fiscal commitments entailed and of the prerequisite that the administration be able to collect and update relevant information on households' composition and income. Those looking at supply-side subsidies alone or considering building public rental housing should be aware that such efforts are often not enough to make housing affordable to the lowest-income groups and are likely to entail long-term budgetary obligations. The cost and effect of subsidies should also be considered when the owner is a public housing authority, another type of governmental entity, or a nongovernmental organization.

Hidden or unpredictable subsidies, such as interest-rate subsidies, should be avoided, and transparent and measurable subsidies should be used instead. Subsidies that create long-term liabilities should be used with care: when a government guarantees loans, the risk should be measured and limited by strict financial control of the beneficiaries. Whether full or partial guarantees, they should be valued at their actuarial value and included in the fiscal budget. Unless there is complete commitment from the government, which is rarely granted, owners take the risk that incentives will stop at some point in the future.

The question then is should other contributors be sought, such as state and local governments, foundations, or employers?

Property management is essential to ensuring that tenants live in safe and decent conditions, as well as providing a resource for owners in rent collection and property maintenance. Governments can take a number of actions including (a) establishing property management institutes for large-scale owners, (b) encouraging those already in commercial property management to start residential arms, and (c) offering training for small-scale or individual landlords.

It is unlikely that a country can or will take all of these steps. However, each step incrementally strengthens the underlying conditions for rental market development. When the underlying conditions are strengthened, the possibility for safe and decent housing increases as does the possibility for investment opportunities.

Taking some of these steps can help a country create a balanced housing policy that addresses the needs of all of its citizens. Although this is not easy, it is clearly essential.

Reference

UN-HABITAT (United Nations Human Settlements Programme). 2003. *Rental Housing: An Essential Option for the Urban Poor in Developing Countries.* Nairobi: UN-HABITAT.

CHAPTER 5

Country Experiences

Brazil*

Rental housing was a very common alternative for Brazilians in the 1930s, as it was considered an attractive investment because of its easy management and good rates of return. This type of housing was especially common for the industrial workers who used to live in the *vilasoperárias*, housing constructed by industry owners for employees and their families. This kind of investment, which typically did not take into account sanitation and hygienic conditions, evolved to become collective housing—under extremely precarious conditions—known as *cortiços*.

After 1940, this environment changed with the advent of the second rental law. The new legal framework brought several bottlenecks for investors, generating additional costs and creating difficulties in recovering property in cases of conflict. This legal change came within a national policy that aimed to protect tenant rights and housing affordability. Another law established a freeze on rents, inducing a significant shrinkage in yearly investment yields, from 12–18 to 4–8 percent (Bonducki 1998). Between 1940 and 1991, more than 20 laws were issued. They promoted minor changes, like the option to increase the rent after two years, but the main principles of the old legislation remained in use.

From 1940 on, national policies targeted industrialization. The creation of the National Finance System in 1964 promoted the growth of urban areas on a model based on acquisition of new houses that reached the middle-income brackets only, excluding the lowest-income population.

Housing policies throughout the 1970s, 1980s, and 1990s focused mainly on construction of new homes, targeting mostly low-middle-income classes. Slum upgrading emerged in the 1990s as a common practice in some states and municipalities as an alternative for improving the life of the poor. This was a consequence of the growth of urban informal occupations and the lack of a centralized policy after the closing of the National Housing Bank in 1986.

---

*The Brazil case study was provided by Anacláudia Rossbach.

The Policy Framework and the Housing Sector

The Ministry of Cities, created in 2003, is responsible for housing policies and programs through its national secretary of housing. In practice, however, rental housing regulations remain under the purview of the economic policy secretary in the Ministry of Finance, who issued regulations on real estate funds (*fundos imobiliários*), and worked on the 2009 review of the rental law. The secretary of economic policy studied and researched many alternatives to improve rental markets, including the possibility of regulating rental conditions on individual contracts, instead of enacting restrictive legislation. No major policy for rental housing has been adopted.

Housing responsibilities overlap at three levels of government. For 20 years there was a lack of centralized coordination. Some states and municipalities developed interesting housing schemes and programs; however, those programs were always limited by budget constraints. Once investments through grants and strong subsidy programs from the federal government started to rise significantly in 2007, states and municipalities had to diversify their complementary programs, especially programs on transitory housing for risky areas and provisory relocations caused by construction works. This is when rental voucher programs started to gain more importance locally.

Municipalities and states must follow national regulations, such as the rental law, taxation, and the national housing finance legal framework. However, they remain relatively autonomous, as a federation, to develop their own programs and local regulations and to decide on their own investments.

Rental's Place in the Housing Sector

According to the 2009 household sample survey Pesquisa Nacional por Amostra de Domicílios (PNAD), only 17 percent of main residences were rented and the home ownership rate was 73 percent. In 2001 in a similar survey, the proportion of rental housing was 13 percent. Table 5.1 shows, however, that ownership rates have not changed significantly: the main movement was between rental and free housing, which does not necessarily mean that rental gained preference over home ownership. In 2009, the income distribution of tenants was very similar to the income profile of all households, showing no exceptional concentration of tenants in any income bracket.

Table 5.1 Brazil: Occupancy Types by Household, 2001 and 2009

Type of occupancy	2001		2009	
	Households (millions)	Share (%)	Households (millions)	Share (%)
Owned	35.0	75	43.1	73
Rented	6.2	13	10.0	17
Free	5.1	11	5.2	9
Other	0.4	1	0.4	1

Source: Based on IBGE data.

Another analysis from PNAD data shows no relevant difference between the shares of rental housing in metropolitan and nonmetropolitan regions or between formal and informal settlements. Looking at geographical dispersion, PNAD data show stable data from 2007 to 2009, with a slight concentration of rentals in the southeast and central west regions.

In 2007, the Ministry of Cities estimated that excessive rent burden for poor families (more than 30 percent of monthly income) accounted for 32 percent, or 2 million households, of the total housing deficit.[1] More than half, or 1.1 million units, was concentrated in the southeast area, especially in the metropolitan region of São Paulo (Ministério das Cidades, Secretaria Nacional de Habitação 2009).

Regulatory Framework

The current legal framework for rent is national Law 8,245 from 1991, amended by Law 12,112 in December 2009. It regulates contracts for residential and non-residential rents. Taxation and economic issues are regulated by general tax and other legislation. Contracts must be in accordance not only with the rental law but also with the new civil code enacted in 2008.

The main features of Law 8,245 and its amendments for contracts are as follows (Presidência da República 1991):

- In residential contracts, owners cannot ask the tenant to vacate, except when the contract is for 30 months or more; in such cases, it will end automatically with no need for advance notice.
- Guarantees accepted are deposits (in cash or assets), *fiança* (personal guarantee), or warranty by a *fiador* (a person who can show proof of income and owns property in the same city), insurance, or the cession of investment funds shares.
- Acceptance of different rental situations includes housing such as cortiços and temporary rentals for vacations, with and without furnishings.
- The option is available to adjust agreed-upon rents periodically and bring them up to market level after three years.
- Rules must be established for subletting.
- Legal procedures must be in place for evictions and other legal actions.

For taxation, specific tributary laws prevail; there is no special benefit or incentive for rental income, which is taxed as any other income. For individuals, the income tax is progressive—15 to 27.5 percent—and some expenses are deductible, such as property taxes and real estate management. Generally, corporate taxpayers must pay 34 percent as income tax and 9.25 percent as "social contributions." Expenses for maintenance, depreciation, and property taxes are deductible.

The Informal Market

Regular studies have shown the importance of the informal markets for rent transactions within the *favelas*, which are informal settlements. Turnover is slightly faster than in the formal markets. Price formation and general market rationale are also different; moreover, each favela has specific features (Abramo 2009, 23).

An analysis of the structure of this market identified demand from two main groups: single male workers and very poor families with a woman as head of household. It also verified that the number of persons per household is much higher in the second group, demonstrating that poorer families live in more crowded conditions (Abramo 2009, 41).

Although the proportion of tenants does not vary with income, the budget burden for low-income families, prevalent in informal situations, is much higher. The lower the income per capita, the bigger is the share of rental expenses in the family budget. This applies to metropolitan and nonmetropolitan regions, in the central-south and north-northeast of the country (Kilsztajn et al. 2009). The same study shows that the share of rental expenses in family income, adjusted for the number of persons in the household, is 29 percent higher for households located in cortiços than for those located in houses or apartments. Cortiços are a form of informal tenement very common in old, dilapidated, central areas in big cities.

In São Paulo, the rent per square meter in cortiços is significantly higher than in formal markets. According to recent data, the average rental cost per square meter in downtown São Paulo is R$28 for units smaller than 10 square meters, whereas, in "noble" areas, the average rental price per square meter is about R$23 for apartments with four bedrooms (Paes Manso 2009).

A very surprising statistic is the gross rate of return to owners and intermediaries, which is, respectively, 1.22 and 2.94 percent of the property's value per month. These figures demonstrate that rental housing in cortiços is a profitable business, especially for intermediaries (Kohara 2009). Cortiços' contracts are also officially recognized in the rental law, which limits subletting rent to five times the rent agreed between the owner and the first renter. This cap is higher than for other types of sublets in which the limit is equal to the rent. This explains, in part, the high rate of return in this type of rental.

Recent Progress and Challenges for the Formal Market

Although the national government has not adopted a rental housing policy, civil society engagement, new legislation, and a history of solving conflicts through the judiciary help to create a safe environment for investors. Some perception of risk in the markets remains from the history of a high level of legal disputes and controversies. But after many years of conflict, the 2009 legislation aligned the judiciary and main stakeholders in consensus on rules and practices.[2] A clear indicator is the number of legal claims related to rental contracts, which decreased by 13 percent between 2009 and 2010.

The 1991 law introduced some benefits for owners, such as the right to charge an "entry fee" at the beginning of the contract and to charge a penalty for early termination. It also brought benefits for tenants, such as the prohibition of entry fees for contract renewals, a preferential buy option in case of sale of the property, and an exemption for extraordinary condominium expenses than were often unduly charged to the tenants.

Another important achievement in the period 2009–10 is the consolidation of real estate investment funds. Although consolidation was made legal in 1993, new issues never amounted to more than R$1 billion (approximately US$600 million). In 2010, the volume of new issues approved by the CVM (Securitization Commission) grew by 238 percent over 2009 and 1,635 percent over 2008. In 2009, the volume of new issues was almost R$3 billion. In 2010, new issues achieved an unprecedented volume of R$9 billion. The reason for the increase was the entry of large investment banks into the sector, increasing yields and liquidity. However, the majority of new issues are for commercial rental (Belleza 2010). Indeed, 2010 was the flagship year for this type of investment funds, not only because of the volume of new issues, but also because of the excellent performance of the portfolio, as its total return averaged 26.9 percent, and the high volumes of transactions.

Low-Income Housing Policy in São Paulo

To widen the range of options for low-income housing, in 2002, the Municipality of São Paulo approved a resolution to establish a rental housing program based on a model of state ownership and rent subsidies for poor families. Under this scheme, the property remains with the government and tenants pay rent according to what they can afford. The first two pilot programs were partially funded by the Inter-American Development Bank.

This program did not evolve further from 2005 to 2010. During this period, the priorities were upgrading of slums, construction of new houses, and development of another type of social housing based on a rental voucher with a structured social component. This new focus can be explained by the high level of investment and maintenance costs required for government-owned rental units, as well as the social issues of vulnerable families and the complexity of the rent setting system. In particular, the government wanted a strong social program to prepare families before they moved from the street or highly vulnerable slums into houses and, during occupation, to provide families with a community-building approach that used social and income-generating activities. In 2007, the municipal housing council approved another program, a voucher system to support rent for socially vulnerable families in privately owned units in the market. Under this program, the municipality pays the full amount of the rent in a private unit for a maximum of 30 months. Eligible families must have a monthly income between one and three times the minimum wage (between US$300 and US$900), with priority given to homeless people, the elderly, victims of violence, families living in risky areas or temporary shelters, and families being relocated by the municipality because of public works.

The program also establishes some requirements, such as minimum health and education commitments, as well as compulsory monthly savings that decrease with family size. The rationale of the program is to provide social support during the 30 months of the rental period and eventually enroll the family in an ownership housing program based on indicators such as savings performance and literacy rate. After the initial 30-month period, an assessment is conducted. If the assessment is positive, the family may apply for a house through a municipal, state, or federal program (see box 5.1).

According to data from the housing secretary, in 2010, after one year of operation, the Parceria Social had benefited 1,012 families with monthly rental vouchers of R$300 (US$175). The first-year outcomes show that 95 percent of children were vaccinated, 85 percent were attending school, 83 percent of pregnant women had access to prenatal health care, and 34 percent of the families were on the list for a definitive housing solution.

Box 5.1 Brazil: From Residential Leasing to "My House, My Life"

In 2009, the government launched its most ambitious subsidies program, "My House, My Life" (Minha Casa, Minha Vida, or MCMV). It significantly raised the level of subsidies for housing to approximately US$25,000 for families earning a monthly income less than three times the minimum wage (US$900) and approximately US$14,000 for families earning between three and six times the minimum wage. The assistance is in the form of up-front subsidies linked to credit.

The program for families earning less than three times the minimum wage requires a significant amount of subsidies and special financial treatment, incurring extra risks for the public bank Caixa. Therefore, the government adapted the existing legal framework for the Programa de Arrendamento Residencial (PAR), a lease-to-own program that had been one of the key instruments for housing policies from 2001 to 2009. PAR had not been successful for several reasons. First of all, because of the amount of subsidies and other measures taken to make housing finance more affordable for low-income families, home acquisition became a realistic option. Next, because leasing was never regulated, the PAR legislation was squeezed between rental and commercial leasing laws. Therefore, the program did not develop in the private sector; instead, it was limited to the publicly financed and privately built housing complexes that remained state property until the end of the leasing contract. Caixa was responsible for monitoring the construction, maintaining the buildings, and carrying out the leasing contracts. Whereas, in PAR, the government, through Caixa, had to keep a real estate portfolio for 15 years; in MCMV, it only acts as a facilitator and enables rapid scaling-up of housing programs. These programs are either fully private or private with local government support.

MCMV also provides opportunities to expand the players in the market, because, in addition to the small and medium-size construction companies that were very active in PAR, the big developers also are now involved in low-income housing. MCMV was launched as part of a rescue plan in the wake of the worldwide crisis that started in late 2008. It aimed to promote the construction of 1 million new houses. By the end of 2010, this target had been met and a second tranche of the program was launched for 2 million more houses.

The Municipal Housing Plan, launched in 2009, considers extending the program to private investment as a way to meet the housing deficit for excessive rental burden. The Municipality of São Paulo is also exploring the implementation of mixed-income rental schemes through a public-private partnership. Such schemes would optimize the use of the existing stock in central areas and create a basis for sustainability in housing projects.

Final Remarks

Rental in Brazil has not been a strong option for housing. The lack of clarity of the legal framework and the dynamics of informal markets kept strengthening home ownership, although, in most cases, on the informal market, home ownership does not mean owning a property title, but merely owning a house.

However, in recent years, with the new legislation and regulations, rental conflicts have decreased and new investment options have evolved that are based on rental contracts. This might enable a safer environment for investments in the future and, therefore, more supply and demand for rental housing.

Despite the recognition of rental housing as an important solution for shelter problems and a relevant component of the official housing deficit (that is, the lack of affordable housing for low-income families), the federal government has not implemented a national framework for social rental housing in Brazil. The main advances in the last decades were the scaling up of slum-upgrading programs and the subsidies program called "My House, My Life" (Minha Casa, Minha Vida, or MCMV; see box 5.1), which represents a historical benchmark in the level of investments by the federal government in housing for the poor.

Although the main policy trend now is new housing construction, rental options are also included in government programs. Voucher systems and public-private partnerships with strong social support should be further developed, especially in high-density metropolitan areas, and involve national, state, and municipal schemes. The national government would remain an important player because it can facilitate local schemes through national legislation, knowledge dissemination, and seed investments.

China*

China has a large construction sector, of which housing represents about one half of the annual volume. Per capita residential space has quadrupled in urban areas between 1978 and 2007 (Man, Zheng, and Ren 2011). The formal home ownership rate is between 84 and 86 percent. Housing affordability has become a major issue in recent years following rapid increases in house prices. The housing sector in Chinese cities needs to cope with the demand pressure caused by migration from rural areas and the aspiration for better quality housing by providing affordable housing both owner-occupied and rental.

---

*The China case study was provided by Kyung-Hwan Kim.

Rental Housing • http://dx.doi.org/10.1596/978-0-8213-9655-1

Description of the Sector

This section provides an overview of the rental housing sector in China. It starts with a description of major shifts in housing policy since the major housing reform of 1998. It then explains the breakdown of housing tenure and the trends in rental housing.

Main Shifts in Housing Policy

Until 1978, most people in urban China were housed by a welfare housing system in which the government or state-owned enterprises produced and allocated housing almost free of charge. Over the next two decades, only a small-scale privatization of public housing took place. In March 1998, a major reform was announced that called for a rapid phasing out of the welfare housing system. This reform encouraged urban residents to buy their current homes from the state-owned enterprises or purchase housing from the market. In fact, all new residential housing units built after January 1, 1999, were to be sold on the open market. State-owned enterprises were prohibited from building any more welfare housing for their employees.

There are several types of affordable housing in China: economic and comfortable housing, price-capped housing, public and low-rent rental housing, and resettlement housing (Ulrich, Hoosain, and Wong 2011). Economic and Comfortable Housing is designed as a way for lower-middle-income and middle-income urban residents to own their own units. It involves government subsidies and profit caps for developers. The primary subsidy vehicle is the allocation of state-owned land at no cost. In addition, projects are subsidized by the reduction or abatement of development costs and fees paid to local governments. Developers' profits are limited to 3 percent. To maintain affordability, the units are generally smaller than unsubsidized apartments. To prevent developers from capturing the subsidy, actual selling prices are supposed to be set so as to ensure that they remain below agreed-on thresholds.

Municipal governments are expected to build and manage rental housing for low- and middle-income residents. Housing for middle-income residents is called public housing. Recently, the central government urged municipal governments to build 700,000 new units between 2011 and 2015, with 300,000 public rental apartments and 400,000 apartments reserved for people displaced because of demolition.

Many municipal governments announced plans to increase the supply of affordable housing, including public rental housing. By 2015, Beijing plans to build one million government-subsidized apartments to house low- and middle-income residents who do not own their homes or who live in extremely small homes. The rental units will be available for households that have a monthly family income of Y 3,000 or less (Y 2,000 for an individual) at a rent level that is approximately 80 percent of the market rate. After renting for three years, tenants will be given the option to purchase the rental unit.

Municipalities face two big issues with rental housing. The first is that they have inadequate resources to finance the construction of rental housing.

The second is that income from land sales and leases represents a large share of municipal revenue. Municipalities try to maximize land sales revenue by allocating more land to market-rate housing and little land to affordable housing. The recent increase in the production of public rental housing was due mainly to the Y 4 trillion stimulus package.

Another issue concerns the location of public rental housing. To reduce costs, housing is built outside of the central cities. For example, in Beijing, most of the new public rental units are built outside the Fifth Ring Road, requiring a long commute to work for residents.

Housing Tenure

China has a very high home ownership rate of 84.3 percent, whereas the share of rental units is just about 10 percent (figure 5.1). The high rate of home ownership reflects the effect of the privatization of housing owned by Danwei.[3]

Despite this high home ownership rate, many homeowners are not happy with the quality of their housing and aspire to upgrade it. The public rental sector consists of a small stock of low-rent public housing. The private rental sector is divided into a formal segment operating on private contracts and an informal segment providing rental housing for workers who have migrated to urban areas for employment.

Trends in Rental Accommodation

From 2011 to 2015, China intends to build 36 million units of affordable housing, covering 20 percent of households. Assuming an average size of 60 square meters, with a land cost of Y 4,000 per square meter and construction cost of Y 2,500 per square meter, this effort will cost Y 2.9 trillion.

Figure 5.1 China: Tenure Distribution

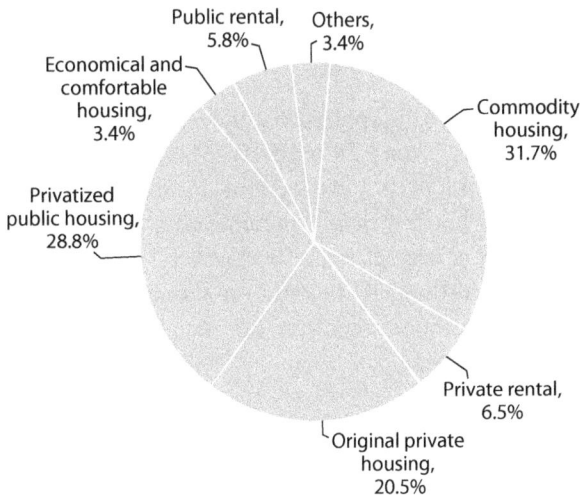

Public rental, 5.8%
Others, 3.4%
Economical and comfortable housing, 3.4%
Commodity housing, 31.7%
Privatized public housing, 28.8%
Private rental, 6.5%
Original private housing, 20.5%

Source: Man, Zheng, and Ren 2011.

The total floor area built between 1995 and 2009 was approximately 8.6 billion square meters, and the total floor space as of 2009 is 13.1 billion square meters (Chen 2010). Assuming an average dwelling size of 70 square meters, these numbers translate into 123 million units built between 1995 and 2009 for a total in 2009 of 187 million units. Chen offers an estimate of urban housing stock at 180 million units. Using data from official urban housing statistics for 2005, Chen estimates that there are approximately 87–90 dwellings per 100 households. Because there are about 200 million urban households, the number of houses in urban areas is approximately 170–200 million. Another study suggests that the urban housing stock is about 150 million. Assuming that 11 percent of households own a second home and 3 percent own three or more homes, there are about 19 million investment units (Rothman and Zhu 2011).

Recently, concern has been growing about high vacancy rates in cites. A controversial report estimates the number of vacant flats at 65 million; however, it is possible that this is an overestimate. Chen (2010) suggests that the maximum vacancy rate is about 5 percent.

Some owners keep their flats off the rental market because the potential rental income is not high enough to compensate for the risks of having a tenant. Gross rental yield is about 3–4 percent (Rothman and Zhu 2011). For example, Huang (2010) estimates the capitalization rate on an 80-square-meter house in suburban Shanghai at 3.8 percent. Wu, Gyourko, and Deng (2012) report that rents are not more than 2–3 percent of house values.

Housing affordability has become a major policy issue in recent years. A large sample survey conducted in 2010 by the National Bureau of Statistics reported a median house price-to-income ratio (PIR) of 7.07 among 265 prefectural cities, up from 5.21 for 2007. Even under the most favorable mortgage conditions, a PIR exceeding 5 makes housing unaffordable. For example, a family spending one-third of its income on a mortgage with a 5 percent fixed interest rate and a 30-year term, would spend 4.63 times its income on principal and interest payments, which does not include taxes and insurance.

The PIR was higher than 5 in approximately 70 percent of the 265 cities, and the average for all cities was 8.79 in 2010 (Man, Zheng, and Ren 2011). Housing affordability problem is most serious in the largest cities. Huang (2010) suggests that the house price-to-income ratio on a small (80 square meters) apartment in suburban Shanghai is about 12. An average household will have to spend two-thirds of its income on servicing the mortgage debt. Given current market conditions, renting the same apartment would cost 40 percent of household income.

Legal Framework

In this section, some aspects of the legal framework governing the rental sector are described. They cover the landlord–tenant relationships, taxation, and financing issues.

Landlord–Tenant Relationships

The legal framework that governs the landlord–tenant relationships in private rental housing is the Urban Real Estate Management Act. The law stipulates that rent cannot be raised during the lease period. When the owner of the rented house plans to sell the house, the landlord must inform the tenant of the plan to sell. The details of the lease are spelled out in the contract.

There is no limit on the lease term, which is determined by a mutual agreement. The landlord can terminate the lease if the tenant is more than a week behind rental payment or sublets the unit without the consent of the landlord. If either party wants to terminate the contract before the lease expires, the initiating party is responsible for paying two months' rent for compensation.

In the case of public rental housing, municipal government regulations set the terms of the lease. The eligibility of tenants is determined by income and other household characteristics. The rent is set at a level slightly over the cost and at a discount from the rent on a comparable private housing unit. The length of lease varies across cities. In Beijing, it is five years.

Taxation

Taxation on urban property is summarized in table 5.2. Various taxes are levied on holding and at transfer. Rental income is taxed, but not reporting or under-reporting of rental income is believed to be widespread. Rental units are not taxed unfavorably relative to owner-occupied units.

Financial Issues

Developers finance projects with development loans, deposits made by home buyers, and developers' own equity.

Financing of public rental housing relies mostly on government funds. According to the Affordable Rental Housing Management Act, four sources may be used to finance public rental housing: 10 percent of land leasing fees of the municipal government, a financial subsidy from the municipal government, a subsidy from the national government, and incomes from the Housing Provident Fund.

Table 5.2 China: Taxation of Urban Property

	Tax	Tax base	Tax rate
Property holding	Urban property tax	Property value	1.20%
	Urban land use tax	Land area	Y 1.5–30/m^2
Sale and capital gains	Turnover tax	Purchase price	2 or 4%
	Stamp duty	Purchase price	0.03–0.05%
	Income tax	Income	20%
	Land appreciation tax	Value added	30–60%
Rental income	Real estate tax	Rental income	18%
	Business tax	Rental income	5%

Source: Based on interviews.

There are no demand subsidies for renters. Some universities and state enterprises offer rental subsidies to their staff as a fringe benefit. The Beijing municipality has announced a plan to provide a housing allowance to 100,000 families.

Conclusion

China has a very high home-ownership rate and the rental market is quite small. In the past, the government dominated the housing market. Since 1978, the policy shifted somewhat away from a social welfare approach to one that used some market-oriented principles that encouraged families to purchase their homes. The government still builds much of the affordable housing. While the rental sector is relatively small, it could provide an alternative to home ownership, which is becoming less affordable, particularly in major cities.

Czech Republic*

Rental housing in the Czech Republic has been viewed as a complementary segment of housing policy, which allowed the government to restitute pre–World War II private rental housing stock. It also helped to prevent wholesale micro-privatization of dwellings in multifamily residential buildings. Rent controls and excessive tenure security have compromised the desirable supply growth of market-based renting. Tenure has not been broadly embraced by the population, which favors home ownership after experiencing decades of Soviet-type public housing. However, the present situation may be pointing to a renewed interest in rental housing.

Housing Policy Framework

Housing policy in the Czech Republic is within the purview of the Ministry of Regional Development, whereas some aspects of housing are handled by the Ministry of Finance (rents, utilities, pricing) and by the Ministry of Labor and Social Affairs (housing allowances). Much of the policy has been decentralized to municipalities, which inherited the state rental housing stock. The government left housing privatization policy to local governments rather than impose centrally mandated micro-privatization. However, the government continued soft rent controls that allowed for small gradual rent increases that lagged behind escalating operating costs. Another cornerstone of the national policy has been the restitution of prewar private rental buildings, which were also subjected to stringent pre-transition rent controls and tenure security for sitting tenants. Vacated and new private dwellings have not been subject to rent and tenure regulations. The government provided housing allowances and mostly supported the growth of home ownership with little support to provision of municipal rental housing.

---

*The Czech Republic case study was provided by Jan Brzeski.

Rental Housing Policy

The government acknowledged the role of the rental housing sector in its strategic intentions. In 1997, it said that the tenure structure corresponded to European standards and that there was no reason to prefer owner-occupied housing to rental housing. However, the continuation of rent controls on municipal and private rental worked against these intentions. Municipalities, which inherited the state rental housing, learned that holding this stock was expensive. The reasons included excessive operating costs, restricted rent increases, tenant protection, insufficient revenue base because of weak fiscal decentralization, and deferred maintenance. Together with the perceived political rewards for enfranchising the sitting tenants, the pressures for give-away micro-privatization eventually reduced the municipal stock by two-thirds.

The government partly compensated for these rental stock losses by providing considerable subsidies for the construction of new municipal rental housing stock. These did not work well, so the program was soon modified and supplemented with subsidies to construction of housing for special-needs households. Recently, the government started another grant support program for construction of social rental flats by various investor categories on the condition of imposing rent increase caps and retaining 10-year rental use with tenant allocation by income criteria. The demand has been slow because of economic difficulties and low profitability for would-be investors.

The government did support rental tenure by allowing for in-kind restitution of prewar private rental buildings, although it retained rent regulations for the inherited tenants. However, these controls did not apply to vacated and newly supplied private dwellings. Consequently, the private rental stock became polarized into two segments with starkly contrasting regulatory regimes. This led to numerous landlord–tenant disputes that tarnished the reputation of restituted landlords and private rental tenure, thus undercutting much of the positive outcome of the policy on preserving a mix of tenure forms.

Housing Stock Composition

According to the preliminary results of the 2011 census, the total occupied housing stock is about 3.9 million dwellings. The country has retained a somewhat heterogeneous housing stock of tenure mix, with a variety of forms in both the home ownership and rental sectors. According to the preliminary results of the 2011 census, the ownership rate reached 81 percent (40 percent single-family, 12 percent coops, and 29 percent condominiums), while the proportion of tenants declined to 19 percent.

The 2008 formal, registered composition of the housing stock showed 77 percent home ownership and 23 percent rental. The home ownership sector had the following typology of dwellings: single-family, 39 percent; cooperative, 16.5 percent; condominium, 21.5 percent. The rental stock was about 950,000 dwellings, of which rent-controlled municipal dwellings numbered 450,000. The private rental segment had about 500,000 dwellings, of which 300,000 were rent controlled and 200,000 had market rents. Ten percent of rental housing stock consisted of municipal rentals, including both the residual of the inherited pre-transition stock and that built during the transition period. Private rentals, including both restituted prewar buildings and formally rented cooperative and condominium dwellings, constituted 13 percent of the stock.

Rental Housing Regulatory Framework

The legislative basis for rental housing consists of the civil code and renting regulations applicable to both municipal and private rented dwellings (Act on Unilateral Increase of Rents). It also includes social protection regulations on housing allowances (Law on State Social Support). Rent control regulations have been challenged by landlords in the country's constitutional court, including the European Court of Human Rights in Strasbourg, France, which instructed the government to mitigate the regime. The ongoing deregulation of rents will require an overhaul of landlord-tenant relations as the number of disputes is bound to rise and with them the need for expedient dispute resolution mechanisms that are faster and cheaper than the court system The system of housing allowances will likely be overhauled as well.

Private Renting

Market rent setting with little security of tenure is allowed only for vacated or newly supplied dwellings; however, the low rents enjoyed by the sitting tenants discourage most of them from vacating. Consequently, a dual tenancy system has been operating within the private restituted rental buildings: (a) inherited tenants enjoying low rents and high tenure security with no incentive to move (see the Social Renting paragraph) and (b) new market tenants paying market rents without excessive tenure security and, in effect, cross-subsidizing the other tenants. This regime makes the landlords strive to stop subsidizing and get rid of the inherited tenants to put the vacated flats on the free market. Consequently, private rental housing has developed an ill reputation for being insecure and expensive, and thus prone to landlord–tenant disputes.

In 2011, six years after the initial proposal, the policy makers agreed to deregulate rents in both private and municipal rental buildings as part of a plan to shift these dwellings to market-level rents. This is being facilitated by rental maps completed by the end of 2011 for 639 cities and towns with populations over 2,000. The maps function as market reference instruments supporting landlords and tenants in rent negotiations, thus helping to minimize disputes. Various experts contend that there is not enough hard market evidence (typically from landlords) to prepare the maps, which call for the use of supplementary expert panels. This may compromise objectivity. Nevertheless, the maps were completed by the end of 2011. By the end of 2010, some 700,000 dwellings had already been deregulated and the remaining 300,000 are expected to be deregulated by the end of 2012.

Social Renting
State or regional regulatory or housing policy framework does not exist on public housing management and sale. Given the multitude of more than 6,000 municipalities, national rent controls have petrified municipal renting, as the sitting tenants can retain their considerably low-rent subsidies by simply staying put and not moving. Many inherited tenants are quite well off, so there is a frequent disconnect between social housing goals and its beneficiaries (i.e. rents do not grow with tenant incomes), which results in a considerable mis-targeting of social policy. There is little formal mobility in this sector, which is gradually experiencing dilapidation. Few dwellings become vacated and those that do are quickly allocated to needy households on social waiting lists. Paradoxically, some informal mobility in this stock has been taking place mainly through informal—actually illegal—subletting with formal tenants receiving untaxed rental income. This should change with the rent deregulation and the necessary modification of housing allowances.

Taxation Regulations
Personal income-tax law recognizes the category "income from rental," which can be submitted to simplified or regular taxation regimes, both taxing income at 15 percent. The simplified regime allows a standard deduction of 30 percent covering all kinds of expenses. The regular taxation regime foresees the use of itemized cost deductions including depreciation allowance, which for residential apartments and buildings is 30 years (3.33 percent per annum). One may net these losses against other income sources in a given year, such as salaries, business income, and capital income. Losses may be carried forward for up to five years. Mortgage interest deductibility is not available to landlords who use the regular tax regime, as it pertains only to owner-occupiers. Strangely, it is available to those who rent informally as they pretend to be owner-occupiers.

Housing Allowances
Tenure-neutral housing allowances were introduced in 1996 to provide assistance to low-income tenants, but have also been used by some tenants and owners who have low cost-to-income ratios. Many private rental tenants with market rents do not qualify. Given that many municipalities did construct new, state-subsidized social housing stock and given the continued rent controls, there has been less pressure to increase the role of housing allowances in municipalities. There was an attempt to introduce state cofinancing of housing allowances, but it was resisted by most municipalities. The system has low take-up, with the number of applicants about half of those eligible. The reasons lie in low, controlled rents, social stigma, information gaps, rational calculation, lack of skills, as well as in deficient allowance design based on notional rather than actual housing expenditures. In 2007, a modified formula was introduced, still retaining the use of notional housing expenditures, albeit changing with the pace of rent increases through deregulation. Once the ongoing rent deregulation is completed, there is

likely to be an overhaul of housing allowances as the need for them is bound to grow with the level of deregulated rents in both municipal and private rental segments. Their design will have to respond to spatially differentiated rents so that actual rents will have to be factored in.

Financial Issues in Private Renting

Three subsegments of private renting are (a) restituted rental dwellings occupied by inherited tenants benefiting from excessive rent controls, (b) restituted rental dwellings occupied by new tenants paying market rents, and (c) privatized apartments and cooperative dwellings rented at market rents, sometimes informally. Given that the third subsegment has attracted a considerable number of individual investor–landlords, and consequently a strong growth in supply, rent increases have not been as spectacular as price increases during the recent decade. This trend has made renting more afford-able relative to home ownership, especially among young housing starters who strongly correlate with this tenure form. This tenant category often views private renting as the first, transitional step in their housing career. The most important financial effect in private renting activity is bound to be the unfolding deregulation of rents during 2011–13. Some 750,000 rental apartments will be up for rent renewal at market rates, and the government has been preparing indicative rental maps.

Private Rental Investment

Private rental investments have grown during the past decade thanks to the attractive yields. Small investors have been drawn also by the more liberal rental regulations and by the relatively favorable incentives in taxation of personal rental income. The government wants to attract developers by offering state guarantees for loans to those who develop rental housing. The recent decade's strong growth in housing prices, faster than rents, has reduced gross yields from the very attractive levels of 7–8 percent to the rather meager 3–4.5 percent. The present inflation level is about 2 percent. In 2012, yields on government 10-year bonds were about 4 percent and medium-term bank term-deposit interest rates were 3–4 percent. These rates may grow again after the rent deregulation reform is completed.

Financial Issues in Social Renting

Management of municipal rental buildings under the rent control regime faces the typical problems of insufficient financing of capital repairs and modernization, which has been one of the reasons for municipalities to sell off the loss-riddled stock. Upon completion of the ongoing rent deregulation, the cost–coverage principle is likely to become the binding operating mode for management of the stock, including increased role for housing allowances and energy-efficiency capital repairs with some European Union funds. One may expect more mobility within this stock, which should free up more vacant dwellings to be allocated to targeted social housing waiting lists.

In addition to the municipalities that manage their rental dwellings and successively sell off their old inherited dwellings, there is a small nongovernmental organization (NGO) social housing community engaged mostly in temporary intervention housing for vulnerable and low-income households. These are mostly financed through government grants and, to some extent, by the donor community.

There is an ongoing policy debate about attracting nonprofit operators and developers, such as housing associations, to build and manage social rental stock while exposed to market risks. The government is also experimenting, through a pilot project, with using parts of the private rental stock for some social policy beneficiaries. The concept is to entice private landlords with guarantees covering the risks and costs of nonpayment of rents, dwelling damages, and dispute resolution. Municipalities would request that landlords enter into long-term contracts at below-market rents supported by the guarantees. The allocation of targeted tenants is to be made by municipalities and NGOs engaged with particular household categories.

France*

The orientation of housing policy in France is underscored by two general principles:

- The "enforceable right to housing," which was made a law in 2007. The "right to housing" means having access to and remaining in decent housing. "Enforceable" means that eligible households that do not get a unit may sue the state. A number of mechanisms, such as low-rent housing, housing allowances, and *Fonds de Solidarité Logement* (FSL), exist; however, local authorities are not able to guarantee the availability of a housing unit for those in urgent need. The number of homeless was recently estimated at 133,000 and that of individuals without a personal dwelling at 685,000.
- Freedom of choice in housing, including tenure, type of housing, and location.

These two principles—the right to housing and freedom of choice—require a sufficient supply of housing, in quantity and quality, as well as in diversity of tenure and social mix. This implies avoiding the concentration of low-income households in social housing and underserved areas. As part of this policy, the law on solidarity and urban renewal (2000) requires that any municipality (except for those with fewer than 3,500 inhabitants, or fewer than 1,500 in the Paris area) belonging to a large urban area (more than 50,000 inhabitants) have no less than 20 percent social housing; those who have less and do not increase the proportion quickly enough are subject to a special tax.

---

*The France case study was provided by Claude Taffin.

Rental Housing • http://dx.doi.org/10.1596/978-0-8213-9655-1

General Overview

In mid-2009, the housing stock consisted of 33.1 million units. Of the total, 9.6 percent were secondary homes and 6.4 percent were vacant units. Some 58 percent of main residences were owner occupied, 37 percent were rented (unfurnished), and the remaining 5 percent were occupied free of rent, rented furnished, or sublet. The shares of social and private rental are very close. Statistics fail to identify in the stock the few subsidized units that are owned by private landlords. Similarly "other social housing" includes all units owned by local authorities (figure 5.2).

Home ownership increased rapidly in the 1980s, from 46 percent in 1978 to 54 percent in 1988, and more slowly thereafter. The private rental sector decreased in the 1980s but has since recovered. The social rental sector grew steadily but slowly before the enactment of the above-mentioned laws. The lack of affordable housing made it necessary to increase the supply.

In 2010, the total benefits, including direct and indirect subsidies, received by the housing sector amounted to €40.6 billion, which was 2.1 percent of gross domestic product (GDP). Direct subsidies (housing allowances) had the largest share (€16.2 billion) (CGDD 2012).

Tenants in the private and social rented sector may benefit from a housing allowance. So may home buyers with a debt burden. The total number of beneficiaries was 6.1 million at the end of 2010:

- 5.6 million households (20 percent of all households), among which 5.0 million are tenants (43 percent of all tenants) and 0.6 million are homeowners
- 0.5 million persons living in hostels.

Figure 5.2 France: Distribution of Rental Stock by Type of Owner, 2009

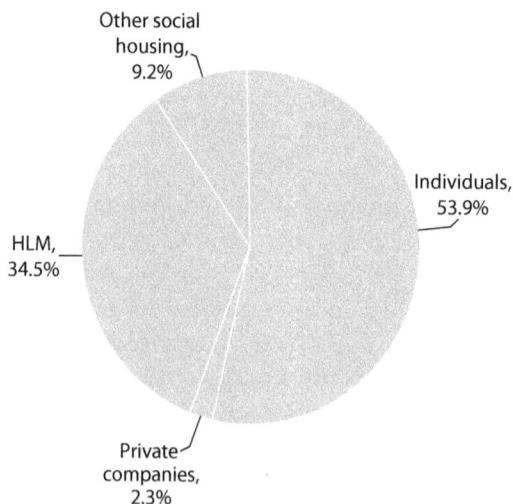

Source: Institute National de la Statistique et des Etudes Economiques (INSEE).
Note: Main residences only. HLM = Habitation à loyer modéré (moderate rent housing).

The amount of the allowance for tenants is directly based on the calculation of the share of the housing expense to be paid by the household: a "rate of participation" is applied to the household's resources. The amount of the subsidy is thus equal to the difference between the eligible expense (the rent up to a maximum level plus a lump sum for utilities) and the household's participation:

$$\text{Allowance} = \text{Rent} + \text{Charges} - \text{Participation}$$

The amount of allowance varies with income, as the participation increases with income; the participation is also lower when the size of the family is larger and it increases with rent (Amzallag and Taffin 2010).

Housing allowances are cofinanced by the state budget (33 percent), the social security budget (the largest share, 51 percent), and the employers' fund (16 percent). The housing allowance is an important component of the "social security net" and a heavy countercyclical financial burden to the housing budget, leaving little margin for other housing policy goals.

The Private Rental Sector

More than 95 percent of the private rental sector belongs to individuals. Low return and heavy management costs have been causing disinvestment among institutional investors for several decades. Most of these landlords own only one or two units. Unbalanced tenant-landlord relationships and heavier taxes have also caused private landlords to sell their property. As a consequence, the private rented stock decreased steadily, losing 1 percent each year in the 1980s, before efficient tax incentives were put in place.

Regulation of Tenant-Landlord Relationships

After rent control was partly lifted in 1948, tenant–landlord relationships were not regulated until 1982 (through the "Quilliot" law) after two changes (the "Méhaignerie" law in 1986 and the "Mermaz-Malandain" law in 1989). Equilibrium seems to have been reached, with the following main features:

- The rental agreement must be in written form; its duration is three years when the landlord is an individual, six years when it is a company.
- The landlord can terminate the lease only when it has expired and only in a limited number of cases (own occupation, sale, etc.).
- The rent is freely set in all new leases (newly rented unit or new tenant); it is pegged to the "reference rent index" during the three- or six-year lease. The reference rent index is equal to the average of the last 12 consumer price indexes. When the lease is renewed with the same tenant, the reference rent index also applies. The rent can be adjusted to reach the level of similar units in the neighborhood only if it is far below market level; in the Paris area, such increases are limited to half the gap. Limited increases are also permitted when improvements are made.
- The law precisely defines which expenses (maintenance, utilities, etc.) will be paid by the landlord and by the tenant.

Taxation of Rental Housing

Any individual receiving income from a rented housing property has to pay two specific taxes:

- Income tax: Rental income is added to a taxpayer's other incomes. In 2012, the marginal rate is 41 percent. The expenses are deductible, including interest payments, maintenance, and management costs. This was designed to take into account depreciation and the few expenses that may not be deducted directly. When the net taxable rental income is negative, the deficit reduces the total taxable income, up to a maximum of €10,700. Any additional deficit can be imputed on the rental income of the next 10 years. If the rental income is less than €15,000, the landlord may choose to deduct a flat 30 percent, regardless of what his real expenses are.
- Social taxes: They represent 13.5 percent of net taxable income in 2012.

Companies pay corporate tax at the flat rate of 33 percent. Social housing companies are exempt for their social rental activity.

Compared with rented units, owner-occupied main residences benefit from three advantages:

- They are exempt from capital gain tax
- Their value is reduced by 30 percent in the calculation of the wealth tax
- Imputed rents are tax-free.

Tax Incentives for Investors in Rented Housing

Several schemes have been introduced since 1984 to encourage individuals to invest in newly built rental housing. Their major requirement was that the property should remain rented for a minimum period of time, between six and nine years. Some of these schemes had maximum rents and maximum incomes for tenants; some had only maximum rents and some did not have any income ceiling.

Two kinds of schemes can be distinguished, according to their mechanism:

- "Quilès-Méhaignerie" from 1984 to 1997 and "Scellier" (since 2009) consist of a deduction from income tax equal to a proportion of the investment, spread over a few years. In 2011, 13 percent of the investment could be deducted over nine years; there is a purchase price limit (€300,000) and a maximum rent but no maximum income. The deduction is 22 percent for energy-efficient buildings.
- "Accelerated depreciation" was used between 1996 and 2009.

In recent years, between 50,000 and 100,000 units per year were sold to investors under these schemes. This represents up to two-thirds of developers' housing sales. The schemes proved to be the most efficient (in terms of number of units sold) when no rent or income limit was imposed on investors. The main issue is the location of the investments: because sometimes rates of return are higher in cities where demand is low, although this seems counterintuitive. In these cities, the parameters have been changed several times to adjust supply and demand. Despite that, when the crisis burst out, several developers had unsold inventories in small cities; they were finally sold to social housing organizations.

These schemes probably have an effect on prices because many programs are targeted toward investors: households tend to overestimate the tax benefit they get from such schemes and may not pay enough attention to the price they pay. They also underestimate the risk they face of suddenly losing the tax benefit if the property is not rented in due course and during the required minimum period of time, or if they do not make the expected profit on resale. In some cases, significant numbers of similar units in the same neighborhood appeared on the resale market at the same time after the minimum rental period. This occurs because of the existence of a price ceiling (€300,000), which tends to concentrate the developers' supply on standardized units such as one-bedroom units in the Paris region, two-bedroom units in other large cities, and three-bedroom units elsewhere.

Social Rental Sector
In January 2011, the stock of social rental housing was 4.6 million units, 13.6 percent of the total housing stock. Three subsectors can be distinguished: the "very social" sector, for the lowest incomes; the central and dominant "standard" social housing; and the "social-intermediate" sector, for the highest incomes.

Social landlords are HLM (*habitation à loyers modéré*—low-rent organizations) and, for a small proportion (5 percent), SEM (*sociétés d'économie mixte*, or semipublic companies). There are two distinct families of HLM: OPH (*offices publics de l'habitat*) are closely linked to local authorities, "communes" or "départements," and ESH (*enterprises sociales pour l'habitat*), which are limited companies with some limitations on their benefits and the obligation to reinvest it in social housing.

All social landlords are eligible for the same loans and subsidies and have the same constraints: a maximum rent and a maximum income for tenants for an unlimited period, depending on the way the program has been financed. Allocation procedures allow financers, such as states, local authorities, and employers, to propose a certain proportion of candidates as tenants in the program that they helped finance.

Once in the premises, tenants have an indefinite right to stay, provided they pay their rent and behave in a decent way. When their income becomes higher than the maximum level allowed, they have to pay an additional rent; in rare cases, they may have to leave the premises.

In markets with high demand, social housing rents can be less than half of the private ones, which entail waiting times that reach 10 years on average in Paris. This rent level requires several layers of subsidies and often cross-subsidization with amortized programs. These aids include the following:

- The benefit of the value added tax reduced rate on land purchase and construction works (5.5 percent instead of 19.6 percent in 2012)
- An up-front grant, totaling between 2.5 and 16.5 percent of the cost; this is higher for purchases of existing buildings and for programs targeted to very-low-income households
- A 25-year property tax exemption, as opposed to 2 years for new buildings in general
- The benefit of an off-market loan by the "Caisse des Dépôts et Consignations" (CDC) guaranteed for free by a local authority.[4]

Most programs benefit from additional subsidies from local authorities and from the "Housing 1 Percent."[5] As of 2010, the total present value of all these subsidies covered more than 45 percent of the cost of a program.

Financing of "standard" social rental housing is done through loans that are:

- Very long term (40 years for construction, 50 years for land)
- Distributed only by CDC and funded by short-term deposits on "A" savings booklets
- Available at a (uniform) rate of 2.85 percent (in December 2011) equal to the interest paid to "A" booklet savers (2.25 percent) plus a 0.6 percent margin.

Deposits on "A" booklets are tax-free and are guaranteed by the state, but they have a maximum amount of €15,300. About 80 percent of French people own an "A booklet," and the total deposit amounts to €215 billion (as of December 2011). The interest rate is now set according to inflation and short-term interest rates under the supervision of Banque de France.

Conclusion

Despite the support to home ownership posted by most governments, the housing stock still has a large rental sector, which is rather balanced between the private and the social sectors, because both receive a significant part of the housing subsidies. To ensure the supply of private rental housing after institutional investors massively withdrew in the 1970s and 1980s, generous tax incentives have been granted to individual investors. This costly housing policy (more than 2 percent of GDP in 2010) is at a crossroads. Indeed, direct subsidies, which are the most important component of housing subsidies and benefit more than 40 percent of tenants, are part of the welfare system and can be reduced only marginally.

Germany*

Germany has one of the lowest home ownership rates in the world. It now reaches only 43 percent and is rising slowly. This is because of several factors: the population is concentrated in urban areas, there is no cultural bias for

---

*The Germany case study was provided by Claude Taffin. It is mostly based on ANIL (2006), Kofner (2009), and Kemp and Kofner (2010).

home ownership, tenants enjoy a high level of protection, and rental investment has long been favored by the tax law through accelerated depreciation. The rental sector offers a wide range of dwellings at moderate prices. Buying a house is expensive: the house price-to-income ratio is between 6 and 7, which is much higher than in France or the United Kingdom (where it is 4–5). Moreover, the lending standards are conservative, with a loan-to-value ratio of 60 percent.[6] Therefore, first-time buyers are older than elsewhere and a large number of German households choose to remain tenants for their whole life, although they could afford to purchase a home.

The Housing Stock

The German housing stock amounts to 38.7 million units, of which 35.9 million are main residences. The large rental sector (23.6 million units) is dominated by small private landlords. Fewer than 1.7 million units have their rent capped and are reserved for low-income households. Since the termination of privileged tax status for low-income housing companies in 1989, this social housing stock may belong to any type of landlord, whether a public or private company or an individual.

The housing stock is newer than in most European countries. After World War II, a massive reconstruction effort was undertaken over three decades. Some 18 million units were built between 1949 and 1978, and 72 percent of the present stock was built after 1948. In the years following the reunification of Germany in 1989, the former the Federal Republic of Germany had to accommodate migrants from the former German Democratic Republic and other communist countries. One million units were built in the early 1990s to address their needs. Since then, the rhythm of construction has slowed considerably: 578,000 units were built in 1997, and only 248,000 in 2006.

The population recently started to decline, and this phenomenon is expected to accelerate in the coming decades. The aging of the population is heightened by the low birth rate. However, the number of households is still slightly increasing and should not decrease until 2025. This does not mean that there will soon be no more housing needs. Germany is experiencing significant internal migrations that increase regional imbalances. Housing deficits in some metropolitan areas contrast with high vacancy rates in others.

Ownership Structure

Small private landlords own the majority of the rental stock: 58.5 percent (figure 5.3). According to a survey published in 2007 by Germany's Federal Ministry of Transport, Building, and Urban Development and quoted by Kofner (2009), old-age provision and tax deductions played a big role as investment motives, not yield prospects or resale intentions. The fact is that only 41 percent of landlords were making a profit from their property and only 21 percent in eastern Germany. Among the private landlords who invested between

Figure 5.3 Germany: Distribution of Rental Housing Stock by Type of Landlord

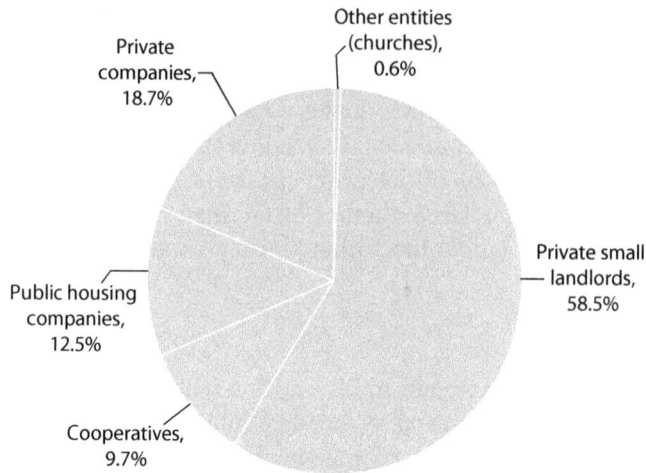

Sources: Droste and Knorr-Siedow 2011; Kofner 2009.

2002 and 2004, the major part of the investment was equity capital for 63 percent, bank credit for 19 percent, and subsidized credit for 10 percent.

Public landlords are mostly municipal housing companies. Although they have no specific legal form, most of them are limited companies. They all have statutory territorial restraint. They are subject to the same tax and rental laws as their private competitors. After playing the role of social housing provider, they now have an ambiguous mission between general interest and profit making. Some of them are even traded, and the city is their main shareholder.

Cooperatives own more than 2 million units (10 percent of the rental stock), half of them in the eastern regions. They are an intermediate form of tenure between ownership and pure rental. They are closer to rental because members of the cooperative who leave their units will get only the present nominal value of their share, but will not receive a capital gain. Some 97 percent of cooperatives are members of GdW (Federal Union of German Housing Companies). GdW is the nationwide umbrella organization for all institutional investors, including housing cooperatives, municipal and other public housing associations, and private housing companies.

Private institutional investors may adopt a variety of legal forms. There are real estate investment trusts in Germany, but they are not allowed to invest in housing stock built before 2007. Open and closed-end funds invest very little in housing.[7] The most important investment vehicles are public limited companies and foreign legal structures.

Since 1997, a considerable part of the public housing stock has been sold to private investors. It includes the housing stock owned by public companies (the postal service and federal railways) and municipal public housing (from Dresden to a U.S. pension fund, for example). If the sellers are clearly motivated by budget considerations, the goals of the investors are less obvious. Short-term capital gains are unlikely, but in the longer term some gains may be expected from sales to sitting tenants. A stable and decent rental return (4.2 percent in 2009, according to the Investment Property Databank), strongly leveraged by very low interest rates (between 2004 and 2006), and a potential increase because of a more professional management are probably the main motivations.

The Legal Framework

The basis for all lease agreements regardless of the landlord—individual or company, public or private—is the civil code. The lease is necessarily indefinite. Apart from noncompliance of the tenant (nonpayment of rent, damage to the property, or antisocial behavior), the only legitimate reason a landlord can invoke to terminate the lease is personal occupancy. However, even here it may be difficult to make the tenant leave. If the tenant refuses to comply and appeals to the courts, the landlord will not necessarily win, because the judge takes into account the situation of both parties: if the tenant is more fragile than the landlord, the recovery may be long and difficult. In addition, because individual landlords own five rental units on average, the recovery for personal occupation may relate to only a small number of cases. The tenant thus has a virtual right to security of tenure. This safety, coupled with relatively low rents, is the main explanation for the lower appetite for home ownership than in most other European countries.

Selling the rented unit is allowed. The tenant or a designated family member benefits from the right to preempt. In case of default, the landlord may initiate an eviction process. The procedure takes about one year, and the cost to the landlord—including unpaid rents, legal fees, and costs of degradation—often reaches very high amounts. To the greatest extent possible, landlords try to avoid using this procedure.

Rent Setting and Rent Increase

In the unsubsidized sector (90 percent of the rental stock), the initial rent is not free. It must be set based on the local reference rent. This reference is the average of rents for similar units, limited to rents agreed upon or raised in the last four years. Rent tables are available in the bigger cities. The landlord may set a new rent up to 20 percent above the reference rate where there is a housing shortage and up to 50 percent above in other cases. In an ongoing rental contract, the reference rate is a strict upper limit: no increase is allowed as long as the rent is higher than the reference rate. There is an additional restriction on rent increases: landlords may not raise the rent by more than 20 percent in three years. The main role of this cap is to limit the rent increases when a social unit loses its status because the agreement has ended. It smoothes the transition to market level by the social rent. Extra rules apply for rent increases after modernization, in particular energy conservation works known as "green investment."

Tax Treatment

All investors, regardless of their status—individual or company, subsidized or not—may deduct from their rental income 2 percent of the value of their investment during a period of 50 years from its acquisition (2.5 percent during 40 years for older buildings). This scheme applies to all investments, including second-hand purchases, which means that this 50-year period is reset every time the property is sold. These characteristics make taxation of rental income much more favorable than in most other countries. Nevertheless, the system was still more favorable before 2006, when accelerated depreciation was replaced by linear. Introduced in 1951, withdrawn in 1973, and then re-introduced in 1977, accelerated depreciation was a major incentive to invest in rental housing. The scales were reviewed several times. In the last scheme (2004–05), the depreciation rate was 4 percent during the first 10 years, then 2.5 percent for 8 years, and 1.25 percent during the remaining 32 years. The total number of 50 years has been unchanged since 1951. Investors in residential real estate also benefit from a tax exemption on long-term capital gains (10 years).

Social Housing

The regulation of social housing is included in two housing laws. Between the first (1956) and the second (2001), the target groups were reduced from "a wide realm of the society" to "those who could not otherwise acquire adequate housing on the markets" (Droste and Knorr-Siedow 2011, 37). More precisely, the income cap was brought down from the fourth to the second decile of the household income distribution.

Another significant step occurred in 1990, when social landlords lost their privileged fiscal status. Investment by ordinary players, such as nonspecialized companies or individuals, has developed since then. The constraints of social occupation are imposed only for a period defined by an agreement that is usually much shorter than the previous standard of 35 years, so that the stock of social housing has rapidly melted. Contractual regulation of existing housing capacities occupies a growing place, thanks to the abundance of private supply on markets that is often not under pressure. It also avoids the concentration of contractually regulated social housing in the same neighborhood or in the same building.

Since 2006, responsibility for social housing has been fully transferred to the *Länder* (regions). With 16 regions, it became even more difficult to have a global view than before, when social housing finance was shared between the regional level and one of four regimes at the federal level. Two main systems coexisted. The first included a soft loan, often interest free, granted by the *Länder* through a regional public bank. The agreement on rent levels and eligibility criteria covered a period at least equal to the term of the loan that is 30 years on average. The second system consisted of an operating subsidy granted by the region during the term of the agreement (Ghekière 2007). A recent trend consists of replacing the subsidized public loan by a market loan provided by a mortgage bank with two separate subsidies: an up-front investment subsidy and a demand-side subsidy complementing the personal assistance *Wohngeld*.

Personal Assistance

Founded in 1965, the *Wohngeld* is paid equally by the federal state and the region. The scale takes into account family composition, housing characteristics, and location (in six areas since 1991) and is intended to maintain the payment-to-income ratio (including utilities) in the range of 15–35 percent, depending on household size. It takes into account the rent and so-called "cold" expenses, that is, excluding heating and hot water. Following reunification, a system called "lump-sum housing allowance" (*Pauschalwohngeld*) was established for recipients of social assistance benefits. Its calculation is independent of the rent. Later renamed the "special housing allowance" (*Besonderes Wohngeld*), it has been integrated with social assistance (*Arbeitslosengeld II*) since 2005.

As reported by the Federal Statistical Office (Destatis), some 850,000 households in Germany received *Wohngeld* at the end of 2010. This is only 2.1 percent of households. The figure was 9 percent before the separation of the special aid. This figure is 11 times lower than in France. The fiscal cost of housing allowances accounts for 0.05 percent of GDP in Germany in 2010. This is 15 times less than in France and 25 times less than in the United Kingdom, which are less populated. The differences may be explained by the relatively low level of rents in Germany compared with those in neighboring countries. The affordability gap for low-income households is therefore narrower.

Conclusion

As far as housing is concerned, Germany is an exception in Europe and worldwide, sharing some characteristics only with its neighbors, Switzerland and, to a lesser extent, Austria. Despite regional imbalances, the housing market is much quieter than in most Western economies, because of these three main factors:

- The housing stock is abundant, and housing needs are bound to decrease because of a negative demographic trend.
- The country is highly urbanized (90 percent), but the population is not concentrated in a few big cities: 81 cities have more than 100,000 inhabitants but only 4 have more than 1 million. The largest urban area, Berlin, has less than half the population of Paris and London.
- Rental is the dominant tenure, with stable tenants and long-term investors, institutional or individuals, who accept that they will not maximize their rental income.

These issues allow Germany to escape the booms and busts that affect many other markets. This may not be proof, but it is at least an indicator that the above-mentioned factors are indeed good stabilizers. The problem is that many countries do not have these factors. Instead, the development of a sizeable rental stock would require such volumes of tax incentives that it would be neither affordable nor politically possible in the short term.

Republic of Korea*

The Republic of Korea's rental housing sector is dominated by the private sector as the stock of public rental housing remains small, although it has expanded in recent years. The private rental sector is closely integrated with the owner-occupied market through a unique type of rental system, the *chonsei*.

Description of the Rental Sector

Over the past two decades, Korea has succeeded in eliminating a serious housing shortage by expanding its housing. Between 1990 and 2009, the housing stock doubled, from 7.36 million to 14.68 million, while the number of "ordinary" households (those excluding single-member households) increased from 10.2 million to 13.2 million. The housing supply ratio, defined as the ratio between the number of dwellings and the number of ordinary households, rose from 72.4 to 111 percent during the same period.

Data on the supply of new housing from 1992 to 2010 are presented in figure 5.4. During this period, the annual supply of new housing averaged 528,000, of which 356,000 came from the private sector. The public sector contributed 172,000 units per year on average. The annual average production of rental units was 96,000: 60,000 units produced by the public sector (35 percent of that sector's production) and 36,000 units by the private sector (10 percent of that sector's production). These rental units include rent-to-own units, which are sold to the renters 5 or 10 years after the initial occupation.

Figure 5.4 Republic of Korea: Supply of New Housing by Sector

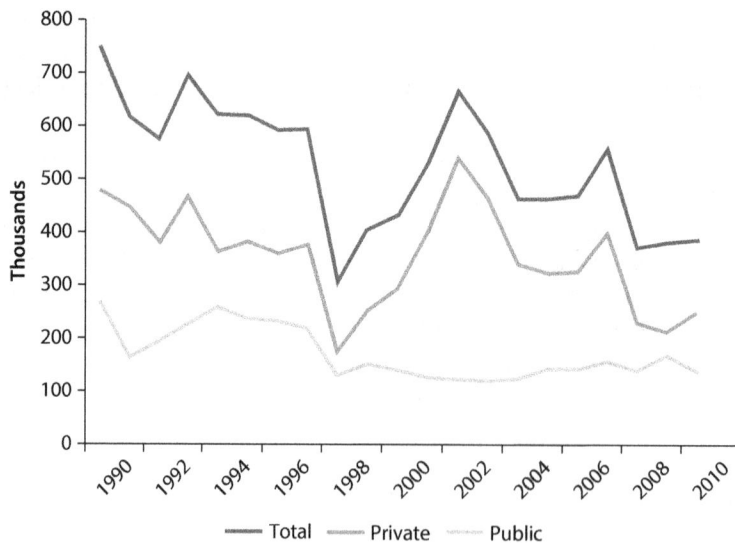

Source: Ministry of Land, Transport, and Maritime Affairs.

---

*The Republic of Korea case study was provided by Kyung-Hwan Kim.

Table 5.3 Republic of Korea: Households by Tenure, 1980–2010

Tenure type and share	1980	1985	1990	1995	2000	2005	2010
Total	7,969	9,571	11,357	12,958	14,312	15,887	17,339
Owner-occupied	4,672	5,127.2	5,774.0	6,910	7,753	8,828	9,390
Share of total (%)	58.6	53.6	51	53.3	54.2	55.6	54.2
Chonsei	1,905	2,202	2,833.0	3,845	4,040	3,557	3,766
Share of total (%)	23.9	23	25	29.7	28.2	22.4	21.7
Monthly rental	1,231	1,893	2,297	1,875	2,113	3,012	3,490
Share of total (%)	15.5	19.8	20.2	14.5	14.8	19.0	20.1
Others	162	350	483	328	406	490	694
Share of total (%)	2.0	3.7	4.3	2.5	2.8	3.1	4.0

Source: National Statistics Office, Korea, 2010 Census of Population and Housing.

Distribution of Tenure

According to the 2010 census, the total housing stock was 14.68 million units (including 800,000 vacant units); apartments represented 8.58 million (58.4 percent of the total).[8] The respective figures for Seoul were 2.53 and 1.49 million (58.8 percent of the total). In terms of tenure, 54.2 percent of all households were owner-occupiers. The home ownership rate was estimated at 61.3 percent because some owners were living as renters somewhere else. The home ownership rate in Seoul was 51.2 percent. These figures are reflected in table 5.3.

Rental tenure in Korea is complex. Monthly rentals with small security deposits, which are a typical lease form in most other countries, make up only a relatively small share of the housing market in Korea. Instead, the most popular lease contract is chonsei, which accounted for 21.7 percent of all households in 2010. Under a chonsei contract, the tenant makes a lump-sum deposit up front to the landlord at the signing of the lease and pays no monthly rents during the lease period. The deposit, which is currently about 50 percent of the price of the house, is refunded in full to the tenant at the end of the lease. The landlord invests the deposit in such a way as to recoup a return comparable to the monthly market rent or higher. The chonsei is unique in that it is not just a rental contract. It is an informal housing loan made by the tenant to the landlord for the right to rent an apartment at no monthly cost. The owner can combine the deposit with his equity and secure a mortgage on the property, if necessary. The level of the deposit relative to the price of the unit is affected by financial market conditions, overall housing market conditions, and the anticipated capital gains.

The Stock of Rental Housing

Public rental housing constitutes a very small portion of the housing stock. As of the end of 2010, 805,841 rental housing units (5.5 percent of the total housing stock) were controlled by the public sector, including the Land and Housing Corporation and local governments. Renters' eligibility for public rental housing is set by the government on the basis of income and family characteristics, and rents are set at a level below market rents.

As in many other countries, individuals who own a small number of rental units provide the vast majority of rental housing in Korea. In addition, 592,000 private rental-housing units were owned by private developers, to be converted to owner-occupied units in 5 or 10 years in a rent-to-own scheme. Private institutional investors, such as real estate investment trusts, are not involved in the rental housing business.

Rental Housing Quality and Rent Burden

The quality of rental housing available on chonsei contracts is about the same as the owner-occupied units. The quality of public rental housing built in recent years is also similar to its owner-occupied counterpart. Some smaller and older units used to be available on monthly rental contracts, but monthly rental leases have become more popular in recent years for all types of housing with all quality categories.

A popular measure of the rent burden is the percentage of income spent on rents. Because chonsei is the dominant tenure type, the chonsei deposit was converted into a monthly rent, using a required yield of nearly 10 percent. In 2008, a monthly rate of 0.98 percent was used. The average rent-to-income ratio is about 23 percent (table 5.4). The figure is higher for lower-income households and in the Seoul metropolitan region.

Reasons for Renting

Those who cannot afford to buy a house may enter into a chonsei contract, which some consider a type of forced savings. Some would-be home buyers remain renters when they expect house prices to fall in the future, which has been the case in recent years. Some homeowners lease out their houses to reside in a different place as renters for job reasons or to send their children to public schools in more popular school districts, in the case of Seoul. The 2010 census reported that 15.5 percent of households in Korea and 18.1 percent of households in Seoul that owned a house were residing in another house as renters.

The Legal Framework

This section describes the legal framework governing the rental-housing sector such as tenant protection, taxation, and financing.

Table 5.4 Republic of Korea: Rent-to-Income Ratio by Income Group and Region
percent

	Low income	Middle income	High income	Average	Metro Seoul	Six large cities	Provinces	Korea, Rep.
2006	36.3	20.7	18.5	22.9	25.3	20.1	18.5	22.9
2008	30.9	21.4	20.3	22.8	26.1	19.5	16.4	22.8
2010	31.1	21.4	21.0	23.1	26.4	19.4	16.2	23.1

Source: Korea Research Institute for Human Settlements.

Tenant Protection

The Tenant Protection Act is the main legislation governing private rental contracts. The standard contract period is two years, and the tenant does not have a right to renewal of the lease. There is a 5 percent cap per year on contract rent at renewal. The act also provides for protection of the chonsei deposit up to a certain limit, if the tenant reports the starting date of the lease. At the time of writing, there was debate over the revision of the act to introduce a provision for automatic renewal and a ceiling on the rate of rent increases. The process of eviction and repossession follows the civil law. The property rights of the landlords are protected, although the legal provision tends to favor tenants.

Taxation

Rental income is taxed at the same rate as other incomes. The maximum rate is 35 percent, and there is a 10 percent surcharge called the residence tax. By contrast, since 2002 the implicit income from a chonsei deposit has not been taxed for two reasons: (a) it was deemed difficult to establish the actual cash income and (b) some returns on a chonsei deposit, such as interest income on a bank deposit or dividend on stocks purchase using the deposit, is taxed separately. However, starting in 2011, a chonsei deposit on a house owned by a household that owns three or more houses is taxed. The taxable income is the amount of the deposit in excess of W 300 million multiplied by the interest rate on a one-year time deposit. No deduction is allowed for depreciation or maintenance.

Korea has promoted the concept of one owner-occupied house for each household and discouraged the ownership of more than one house. In fact, Korea has a unique capital gains tax system whereby the tax rate gets higher as the number of houses owned grows. The normal tax rate ranges from 7 to 35 percent, depending on the amount of assessed capital gains. An exemption is granted to long-term (five years or longer in Seoul) owners of only one house worth less than W 900 million. Owners must fulfill a residence requirement, which is three years in Seoul. The tax rate is 50 percent for the second house and 60 percent and up for the third house. The owners of two or more houses as well as those of one house worth more than W 900 million must also pay comprehensive real estate tax in addition to the local property tax. Tax exemptions are granted to those who register as landlords and rent their houses for three years or longer, and the requirements for qualification change over time as government policy changes depending on the phase of the housing market cycle.

Loans and Guarantees

The suppliers of rental housing, including rent-to-own apartments, can borrow from the National Housing Fund (NHF), a government fund managed by the Ministry of Land, Transport, and Maritime Affairs. The Housing Credit Guarantee Fund (HCGF), a government credit-guarantee scheme managed by the Korea Housing Finance Corporation, offers a guarantee for developers that seek funding from private financial institutions.

Loans are made to chonsei tenants toward their deposit, and HCGF provides a guarantee on such loans. NHF and local governments also provide chonsei deposit loans for qualifying moderate-income tenants. The interest rate is set below the mortgage lending rate. On the relatively rare occasions when deposit levels fall, NHF extends loans to landlords to enable them to repay chonsei deposits to tenants. This happened during the Asian financial crisis and the global financial crisis.

Subsidized Public Rental Housing

The first government program for public rental housing was initiated as a component of the 1988–92 drive to build 2 million new housing units. The program consisted of a plan to build 250,000 permanent rental units for the lowest 10 percent in the income distribution. The program ran into difficulty in securing land in the cities and was deemed too costly for government. As a result, the program ended after producing 190,000 units.

Government interest in public rental housing was renewed by the Kim Dae Jung government in 1998. The government announced a plan to build 50,000 national rental housing units by 2002. As the chonsei deposit index increased in 2000, the target was adjusted in 2001 to build 100,000 units by 2003, and later to 200,000 units. These rental units were to be rented for 5–10 years and then sold. According to the 2000 census, 3.3 million households, or 23.1 percent of all households, were living in houses that fell short of the minimum standards; they formed a basis for the rental housing program.

Roh Moo Hyun, then a presidential candidate, made a campaign pledge to build 500,000 rental units between 2003 and 2007. Once elected, President Rho revised the plan to build 1.5 million long-term rental housing units—including 1 million national rental housing units—for a 10-year period. During the 2003–07 period, 560,000 public rental units were built under this program. The rental housing project was financed by the government budget (10–40 percent of the total cost), a loan from the NHF (40–50 percent), and the Korea National Housing Corporation (10 percent). The beneficiary household paid 10 percent. The relative shares varied by the size of the rental units. The cash-flow shortfall became a major reason for the financial hardship of the corporation.

The Lee Myung Bak government modified the public housing program of the previous administration by lowering the annul target for production as well as by increasing the share of low-cost housing for owner occupation. The rental housing program now consists of four kinds of units: permanent rental (to be rented for 50 years), national rental housing (30 years), long-term chonsei (20 years), and rent-to-own (10 years). The target for 2009–18 is to build 100,000 permanent rental units, 400,000 national rental housing units, 300,000 rent-to-own units by the public sector, and 100,000 rent-to-own units by the private sector. The government provides a direct subsidy and a below-market-rate loan through the NHF. In 2012, this was set at a 3 percent interest rate, payable for 20 years after a 10-year grace period. Land that could be developed was subsidized as well. About 336,000 rental units were built between 2008 and 2010. One side effect of the public rental housing drive was that it nearly wiped out the rent-to-own scheme by private developers.

Support to Private Rental Housing Production

The government allocates developable land to the producers of rental housing at subsidized prices. Funding from the National Housing Fund is also available at a subsidized interest rate. In return, the level of rents and the sales price of the units at the end of the lease period are regulated by the government.

Direct Subsidies to Tenants

There is a government program for a rental subsidy for the lowest-income households. This is provided as an integral component of a welfare program, and, for that reason, is considered a cash support to top up the welfare allowance. The introduction of a housing voucher scheme has been discussed in recent years, and the Ministry of Land, Transport, and Maritime Affairs has been promoting it as a pilot project. However, the Ministry of Finance did not allocate even a small budget for the pilot project proposed for 2010 and 2011. The main reason was that the cost of the program, if adopted on a full scale, would be too great.

The Seoul city government introduced a rental subsidy scheme of its own in 2009 and planned to expand it in the future. The voucher program is for those with income less than 120 percent of the minimum living expenses determined by the government each year, and those with income less than 150 percent of the minimum living expenses who are handicapped or in single-parent families. The amount of the subsidy is modest at W 43,000–65,000 per month. The number of recipients in 2011 is expected to be 8,200; the Seoul city government plans to increase that number to 50,000 by 2020.

Conclusion

Private rental sector is experiencing some fundamental changes. Rental housing has long been a residual sector to owner-occupied housing. In recent years, more renters have been renting by choice, so that chonsei deposits and rents have been increasing. This trend is likely to continue as the price of housing stabilizes and population aging proceeds. A key question concerns how the supply of rental housing can be increased to meet increasing demand. Some argue that public rental housing stock should be expanded, but it will be very costly. Another issue relates to making rental housing more affordable. Politicians are in favor of introducing some form of rent control. A national program of housing voucher is being considered.

Mexico[*]

According to the 2010 population census, Mexico has a population of 112.3 million people in 28.6 million households. The need for new housing stock is increasing every year. The demand in 2009 was estimated to be close to

---

*The Mexico case study was provided by Ira Peppercorn and Claude Taffin.

1 million units, but only 600,000 are being built each year in the formal sector. The gap is expected to grow as the growth in households continues to outpace the growth in houses.

According to the 2008 survey on households' incomes and expenses by the National Survey of Household Income and Expenditure (ENIGH), 8.95 million units—approximately one in three—have a major flaw that could affect the health or safety of residents:

- 600,000 are overcrowded (two or more households share the same unit)
- 1.1 million have deteriorated since they were constructed
- 7.2 million, particularly those that were self-built or modified, were built with substandard materials.

An Emphasis on Home Ownership

Although housing policy makers have so far emphasized home ownership, the following factors should be taken into account:

- A large proportion of households have no access to credit.
- Among those who have access, buying a house on the market is unaffordable or affordable only at a great distance from their place of employment.
- Those who live in rural or semirural areas are likely to have no access to mortgage finance.
- After the 2009 global financial crisis, the largest specialized lenders (SOFOLES or SOFOMES), went bankrupt when this sector was, at least originally, the only one to serve some households active in the informal sector. Investors became very wary of the quality of portfolios, bringing private securitization to a halt.

Access to Credit

Some 55.7 percent of households have employment that gives them access to social security (table 5.5)—a necessary condition for acquiring a mortgage. A large proportion of the workforce is in the informal, nonsalaried sector.[9]

Table 5.5 Mexico: Distribution of Households by Type of Employment and Income Level
percent

Minimum wage multiple	Formal employment	Informal employment	Total
0–3	3.9	16.8	20.7
3–6	16.1	16.9	33.0
6–9	3.1	5.5	18.6
More than 9	22.7	5.2	27.8
Total	55.7	44.3	100.0

Source: Fundación CIDOC and Sociedad Hipotecaria Federal (SHF) 2009, using ENIGH 2008 data.
Note: Formal employment means with access to social security; this refers to the situation of the head of the household. This information was available for 24.3 million of 26.7 million households.

Although some lenders will originate mortgage loans to those whose incomes are informal, most will not or cannot. This applies particularly to INFONAVIT and FOVISSSTE, the private and public sectors housing provident funds, which are the dominant players in the market.

Another key determinant of access to the mortgage market is income level. Those at the bottom of the income pyramid earn six times the minimum wage or less. Slightly more than half of the population (53.7 percent) is in this category. Among them, 20 percent have income derived only from the formal sector. They do not have access to a mortgage loan unless they are provided with some type of subsidy, such as CONAVI's Esta es Tu Casa program, which can assist salaried workers who have an income as low as 1.5 times the minimum wage.[10]

The Housing Subsidy System

Mexico's housing subsidy system is focused almost completely on home ownership. The bulk of housing subsidies come in the form of below-market interest rates provided primarily by INFONAVIT (the housing fund for private-sector workers) and FOVISSSTE (the housing fund for public-sector workers), which receive the core of their funding by contributions to retirement accounts. These organizations provide loans with subsidized rates that range from 4 to 10 percent, depending on the borrower's income.

The Rental Sector

Mexico is a good example of a country where the rental housing market is likely larger than it might initially appear. The published home ownership rate is estimated to be 71.5 percent, and the rental rate is listed as approximately 14 percent (table 5.6). However, an additional 14 percent is classified as "other," primarily living in what are considered borrowed dwellings (12.8 percent). It is likely that "borrowed dwellings" are actually rented dwellings for which the landlord or owner does not declare the income.

Interestingly, the distribution of the percentage of owners versus renters does not vary dramatically according to the income scale. Those with the lowest

Table 5.6 Mexico: Distribution of Households by Tenure and Income Level

percent

Minimum wage multiple	Tenant	Owner	Other
0–3	13.0	70.8	16.3
3–6	16.5	66.0	17.5
6–9	14.9	72.1	12.9
9–12	14.1	73.0	12.9
12–15	11.8	79.4	8.8
More than 15	11.4	81.8	6.8
Total	14.3	71.5	14.2

Source: Fundación CIDOC and Sociedad Hipotecaria Federal (SHF) (2009), using ENIGH 2008 data.
Note: Minimum wage equals Mex$1,870 per month, or US$145 in the Federal District for 2012.

income have a 70.8 percent home ownership rate; those with the highest incomes have an 81.8 percent rate. However, those with lower incomes are likely to live in dwellings that are self-built and in poor condition, whether owned or rented.

More than one-third (36 percent) of rental housing is concentrated in three states (Distrito Federal [DF or the Federal District], Mexico, and Jalisco); adding two more (Veracruz and Puebla), one reaches nearly half (46 percent) of rental housing. This is a common pattern in many countries where the centers of the large cities have the highest real estate prices.

Segmentation

The rental housing is, in large proportion, in the informal sector. There is virtually no formal system of large landlords, property managers, and institutional investors like those that exist in other countries, such as the Federal Republic of Germany or the United States. Nor is there any system of social rental housing, or housing that is owned by a governmental or a nonprofit entity and rented to persons who have low income or special needs.

Investors and property developers believe the rental sector is too risky in general and even more so for housing for the middle- and low-income populations. Professional property managers exist only for high-end rental properties. Additionally, there is a perception that tenants will not take adequate care of units and that security deposits could not cover the costs of repairs. There is some activity in formal rental housing at the high end of the market for professionals in the upper-income sector who desire to rent new or relatively new units.

While the rental market is indeed serving middle-income and poor people, this is almost always by small landlords, not by a formal rental-housing sector. The middle-income sector is served by individuals who own fewer than 10 units. The properties are managed by the owners because of the cost and scarcity of professional property management in this sector. The units can vary from apartments in small buildings to rooms in houses. The quality of dwellings in this sector varies greatly from property to property.

For the low-income sector, much of this consists of informal housing, such as single rooms in what can be considered rooming houses, with shared bathroom and kitchen facilities. In central cities, the quality of these units is often poor.

Legal and Administrative Concerns

Tenant and landlord rights and duties are regulated at the state level, and regulations are embedded in the civil code and the Code of Civil Procedure. In 2007, it appeared that they included as being regulated (a) the maximum amount of the initial rent, (b) the setting of the annual rent increase, (c) the amount of the deposit, (e) the initial duration of the contract and its extension, (f) the reasons for terminating it, (g) the preferential rights of the sitting tenant for the new contract, and (h) the registration of the contract. The Code of Civil Procedure establishes the process to resolve disputes and the interpretation of the rules.

Rental laws favorable to tenants were passed in the 1970s. In recent years, there has been a trend toward more favorable treatment of landlords (seen in the civil code reform in 1994). However, according to most potential investors, the legal protection afforded to residents remains a great barrier to stimulating a large-scale residential real estate industry.

The main issue has to do with residents' legal rights in the case of eviction or foreclosure. Some of the experts interviewed noted that the time to resolve such situations had been reduced from three or four years to less than one year, a timeline that they consider manageable. These experts argued that the relevant laws would probably need only minor adjustments, such as a more flexible limit on rent increases (10 percent, or whatever the variation of the consumer price index).

Although there are different perceptions among stakeholders, it seems that in general, (a) the legal system has improved in this area from the landlord's point of view, (b) the system varies from state to state, and (c) although the legal system might have improved, the issue remains that some residents refuse to leave even after a judicial ruling against them because the local authorities may be reluctant to enforce the ruling.

The Tax System

From a comparative standpoint, the tax burden on rental housing is not high compared with many other countries. Yet, avoiding taxation is a key reason that owners do not register or pay taxes on a high proportion (80–90 percent) of rental properties. This does not mean that there is not a written rental agreement: there may be a contract that has not been registered; there may also be a registered contract, but the taxes are not paid. Taxes (property and rental income) are paid for only on an estimated 10 percent of rental units, which roughly corresponds to the market share of institutional investors.

Income Tax

The scale of income tax (*Impuesto sobre la Renta*) has a maximum rate of 30 percent (recently raised from 28 percent). Mexico still has one of the lowest income-tax rates among member countries of the Organisation for Economic Co-operation and Development. On the one hand, this maximum rate is rapidly reached; on the other hand, many personal deductions are allowed for individuals and companies, so that this rate does not necessarily reflect the amount that is actually paid.

Individual rental property owners may deduct a flat 35 percent for their operating costs (standard deduction) instead of real costs: (real) mortgage interest, maintenance, and management costs. Only the property tax (*Impuesto Predial*) is deductible in addition to the standard deduction. No depreciation is permitted.

Legal entities may deduct all the real expenses mentioned above, including insurance premiums, provisions for vacancy, and legal costs. Depreciation is allowed at the (favorable) rate of 5 percent for new construction.

Rental Housing • http://dx.doi.org/10.1596/978-0-8213-9655-1

Because many deductions reduce the effective tax burden, a flat-rate business tax (*Impuesto Empresarial a Tas Unica*, or IETU) was introduced in January 2008. The IETU is a minimum complementary tax that can be compared with the U.S. government's alternative minimum tax. It is due whenever the income tax is less than the amount obtained by applying to the taxable income the flat rate of 17.5 percent (from 2010). The IETU allows full deduction of investment costs and the carrying forward of deficits for 10 years (equivalent to a 10 percent depreciation rate), but interest rates are not deductible. Taxpayers must pay the higher amount of current income taxes or the IETU tax. Therefore, the effect of IETU depends on the personal situation of each taxpayer.

Leverage through credit is a key instrument used to make rental investment profitability comparable with that of other investments. The limited deductibility of interest rates paid (only real rates are taken into account, a current practice in countries with high inflation, which is not the case in Mexico anymore) and the newly created IETU therefore appear to be major impediments to rental investment.

Other Taxes

• Value-added tax (*Impuesto al Valor Agregado* [IVA])

Housing rental is exempt from value-added tax.

• Property tax (*Impuesto Predial*)

The property tax is a local tax. Its amount is based on the value of the property. In the past, only in Mexico DF was a double calculation made, and the tax due for rental units was the higher of the tax based on the rental value and the tax based on the market value. Since 2008, only the market value (according to the cadastre, bank records, or similar transactions) has been used, as in other cities.

There are important differences between the scales applied by the various states: For a "social" unit of Mex\$230,000, the rates vary between a minimum of 0.07 percent in Jalisco and a maximum of 0.90 percent in Quintana Roo. In Mexico DF, the rate is 0.08 percent for homeowners and 0.45 percent for landlords.

• Schedular tax (*Impuesto Cedular*)

Since 2005, the states have been allowed to raise the schedular tax on the rental income of individuals (at a minimum rate of 2 percent and a maximum of 5 percent). Only Guanajuato has introduced this tax (at the rate of 2 percent).

• Transaction tax (*Impuesto sobre Adquisicion de Inmuebles* [ISAI])

Transfer of real estate property is subject to a local transfer tax, the ISAI. In Mexico DF, the rate of the tax increases from 3.2 to 4.6 percent by tranches of value (the first Mex$73,500 is exempt). In addition to the tax, registration fees and notary fees are due; they may amount to up to 7.5 percent of the purchase price.

- Capital gains tax

A capital gains tax is levied for any resale of real estate property except for the main residence, which is the case most often seen in other countries.

Conclusion

Rental housing is an important part of the Mexican housing market. Because of strong tenant protection and unfriendly taxation, this market is mostly informal. Lack of professional management and of ad hoc finance also explains why large-scale investors are virtually nonexistent. There are many countries where the vast majority of landlords are individuals. In Mexico, large-scale investors are particularly necessary because they would increase the supply of multifamily buildings and thus contribute to reducing urban sprawl.

Poland[*]

Poland, like the Czech Republic, but unlike most other post-Soviet countries, has consistently viewed rental tenure as a component of housing policy with strong recognition of labor mobility implications. It restituted the prewar private rental housing stock and it limited the privatization of apartments in multifamily buildings. Excessive rent controls and ineffective eviction procedures have undercut desirable growth of market-based rental supply, while social rental production has been insufficient to meet the demand. Home ownership has been the focal point of the housing policy, resulting in less interest in rental housing. However, the present situation points to a renewed interest in rental housing.

Housing Policy Framework

In Poland, the Ministry of Infrastructure is responsible for national housing policy, but much of policy formulation and implementation has been devolved to municipalities. This includes the transfer of ownership and management of the state rental stock to local governments who then work with the existing tenants. The government has retained the pre-transition features of excessive tenure security and rent controls with an overall ceiling of 3 percent of replacement cost. Another cornerstone of national policy has been the restitution of pre–World War II private rental buildings, which had long been subjected to stringent rent controls and tenure security for sitting tenants. Vacated and new private

---

*The Poland case study was provided by Jan Brzeski.

dwellings were not subject to rent and tenure regulations, although soft rent controls regarding rent review and increase were imposed.

The government is preparing an overhaul of national housing policy proposing to strive toward more tenure neutrality through phasing out interest buy-downs, abolishing housing allowances for homeowners, and enabling tenants in private rental housing to use housing allowances more effectively. The government is also advocating for public-private partnerships in the development of municipal rental housing, although the first attempts have not yet succeeded, mainly because of obstacles in extending municipal guarantees that add to the already high public debt.

Rental Housing Sector in Housing Policy

During the two decades of transition following the overthrow of communist rule in 1989, the successive governments have recognized rental housing as playing an important complementary role in both housing and labor markets, although policy programs have not been perceived to be particularly helpful. An early support program of subsidized financing for the development of rental buildings was abused and discontinued. Another attempt, with more lasting effects, was a program of fostering nonprofit rental housing. The initial "hard" rent controls were modified into a "soft" rent regime focused on rent review and increase, with explicit recognition of landlords' rights to "reasonable profit." Municipalities, which inherited the state rental housing, learned that holding this stock was expensive because of excessive operating costs owing to rent controls and tenant protection. There was insufficient revenue base caused by weak fiscal decentralization and the staggering costs of deferred mainte-nance, creating a renovation gap. Together with the political profitability of enfranchising sitting tenants, the pressures for give-away microprivatization reduced the municipal stock eventually to about 10 percent of the total stock and about 40 percent of the rental stock.

Composition of Housing Stock

Poland's total housing stock amounts to 13.3 million dwellings for almost 15 million households. This stock is composed of a balance of multifamily (48 percent) and single-family (52 percent) dwelling types, reflecting the coun-try's considerable rural population (33 percent of dwellings) and the legacy of single-family suburbs that grew during the Soviet economic period.

The legal composition of the housing stock consists of 75 percent ownership (including cooperatives) and 25 percent rental, with the ownership stock con-sisting of single-family (70 percent), cooperative (17 percent), and condomin-ium (13 percent) tenure types. The functional composition consists of 66 percent owner occupation and 34 percent tenant occupation. The multifamily buildings are managed by municipalities, cooperatives, condominium associa-tions, social nonprofit TBS (Society for Social Housing) entities, and private landlords. Many buildings need capital repairs, renovation, and modernization. The "renovation gap" has grown during the two decades of transition because of rent controls and the unwillingness of privatized tenant-owners to bear the full costs of maintenance and repairs.

Rental Housing Sector

The rental housing sector constitutes 25 percent legally and 34 percent functionally of the housing stock, almost all of it being multifamily dwellings. Individual renting of cooperative and condominium flats, typically informal, accounts for most of the legal-functional difference. Given the even split between single-family and multifamily dwellings, the share of renting in the multifamily stock ranges from approximately 50 to 70 percent within the legal-functional spectrum. Tenant occupation is typically found in municipal, cooperative, and condominium dwellings, in specialized rental buildings of nonprofit TBS entities, and in private rental dwellings, which form the largest segment—legally about 50 percent and functionally about 60 to70 percent.

The social rental sector consists of three segments: (a) municipal rental, including special-purpose dwellings, dormitories, and shelters; (b) nonprofit TBS rentals; and (c) institutional rental, such as for students, military, police, and other government workers. While the municipal rental stock has been diminishing through microprivatization, the state-subsidized nonprofit rental stock has been growing. Today it constitutes almost 10 percent of the multifamily rental stock, while the municipal and institutional rental stock constitutes less than 40 percent. Some new social housing construction has been supported by the state, mostly in the area of purpose-specific dwellings and shelters.

The government introduced a program to foster development of TBS housing targeting "intermediate" households that are shut out from purchasing on the market and from qualifying for municipal social housing. The program produced more than 90,000 dwellings during the 15-year period, did not achieve the anticipated production goals, and recently faced the prospect of discontinued favorable lending. The government is deliberating whether to replace it with a new rent-to-own support program. In the meantime, the government is considering a parliamentary proposal to allow tenants to buy out their TBS dwellings under certain circumstances and at market pricing. Nevertheless, the substantial oversubscription of the TBS program demonstrated considerable pent-up demand for nonprofit moderate rental housing and fostered a new category of rental developer–operators skilled in cost-based production and management of rental stock.

Rental Housing Regulatory Framework

The legislative base for rental housing includes the civil code, the Tenant Protection Act, the Law on Some Forms of Supporting Housing Development, and the Law on Financial Support to Development of Social Premises, Special-Purpose Dwellings, Dormitories, and Homeless Shelters. Rent regulations were adopted at the outset of reforms and imposed on municipal and restituted private rental buildings, allowing for rent differentiation under the 3 percent replacement-cost ceiling. However, local elected councils have resisted rent increases, so that after 20 years the average municipal rent has reached 1.3 percent of the replacement cost. Rent setting and tenure security regulations have been successfully challenged by landlords in constitutional court and in the European Court of Human Rights in Strasbourg, France, which asked the government to mitigate the regime and recognize landlords' right to "reasonable profit."

Private Renting

Since 2007, all private rental dwellings are no longer under hard rent controls, with rents including a "reasonable profit" component. However, there is no definition of how to quantify reasonable profit, so the courts are expected to rule on this issue. Rent increases to levels exceeding the 3 percent replace-ment-cost ceiling must be substantiated by landlords upon tenant request. One of the valid reasons for exceeding the ceiling is now the need to achieve a reasonable profit. Tenants who are not satisfied with a landlord's detailed writ-ten explanation can take the landlord to court, which is a lengthy process. One court ruled that the yield rate on government securities could be used as a reference point for reasonable profit. Valid reasons for higher rent also include inflation indexing and capital cost recovery of up to 1.5 percent per year for construction or acquisition costs, or 10 percent of capital for capital improvements.

The highest risk in private renting is the enforcement of eviction in cases of rent default. The courts are generally opposed to outright eviction of tenants, instructing bailiffs to provide debtor-tenants with either provisional shelter or a social dwelling allocated by the pertinent municipality. Given the genuine shortage of both types of premises, defaulting tenants remain in their dwellings de facto for free. Although the landlord has grounds to demand compensatory payments for rent arrears from the municipality, this appeal must be based on other laws and regulations. Municipalities try to avoid paying such compensations.

The rigid framework of tenant protection and restrictive controls on rent increases provides a breeding ground for disputes, which increases investment risk and, given the weak tax incentives, discourages more investment in private rental housing. These factors contribute to the persistence of informal renting by individuals who do not report their incomes to avoid taxation. The government is trying to entice informal landlords into the formal sector by offering incentives through "occasional renting" by individual apartment owners. The major regula-tory incentive provides for expedient eviction using the tenant's notarized agree-ment to be evicted to a predetermined dwelling. This is tied to the tax registration of the contract, subject to a low flat tax of 8.5 percent. Too little time has passed to draw conclusions about this effort.

Social Renting

Rent reforms have been slow to come, which has led to growing dilapidation of the municipal housing rental stock. There is a general tendency for the poorest-quality stock to be left with municipalities, because tenants have little incentive to take over and renovate. The rent controls imposed by the government on municipalities have immobilized municipal renting because the sitting tenants can retain their low-rent subsidies only by staying, not moving. Many of the inherited tenants are not poor, so the goals of social policy are compromised. There is little formal mobility and buildings have deteriorated as rents do not cover necessary maintenance measures. Few dwellings are vacated, and those that do are quickly allocated to needy households on the social housing waiting lists run by municipalities. Paradoxically, some informal mobility in this stock is taking place through illegal subletting.

Municipalities struggling with the maintenance gap in their stock are finally starting to mobilize more rental income by differentiating rents to better mimic market pricing relationships, but still under the 3 percent ceiling. This has produced a considerable flow of rental income from the highly valuable municipal flats, which now face much higher rents, even if they entail increased expenditures for housing allowances to qualified households. Many municipal tenants do not need housing allowances.

Taxation Regulations

Income taxation of rental income can be applied through one of three regimes: (a) personal income tax (PIT) using marginal tax rates of 18 or 32 percent on net income after deductions; (b) PIT using a flat rate of 19 percent on net income after deductions; and (c) a simplified flat-rate (ryczalt) tax at 8.5 percent of gross income with no deductions for unincorporated business activity. "Natural persons" without incorporated business activity can choose between the first and third regimes, and those with incorporated business activity can choose between the first two regimes. Since 2010, individual homeowners who formally rent out their dwellings occasionally have been able to use the third regime.

In the regimes under which net incomes are taxable, a number of deductions may be made:

- Capital depreciation (1.5 percent for condominium and 2.5 percent for cooperative)
- Property taxes on the dwelling and the land
- Interest payments on mortgage credit used for purchasing the rented dwelling
- Equipment, furnishings, and capital repairs
- Operating and maintenance costs
- Any other costs incurred to generate rental income.

These regimes allow also for pooling rental income with other incomes and for loss carry-forward, with annual losses from capital expenditures on major repairs carried forward at 50 percent over the next five years. Capital gains from the sale of property are tax-exempt after five years of ownership but taxable at a flat 10 percent rate within the first five years of ownership.

Rental Housing • http://dx.doi.org/10.1596/978-0-8213-9655-1

Housing Allowances

Tenure-neutral housing allowance schemes are run and financed by municipalities, although their application to privately renting tenants has been hampered by the informality of many such rentals and by their links to the controlled low-rent levels adopted by municipalities. The schemes are means-tested and quite wide-ranging, with about 30 percent of households receiving them. The allowances are paid to tenants, usually through social assistance administration, and are tested on both income and property holdings. The allowance amounts are subject to limiting conditions regarding dwelling standard and normative rent levels. In its recent drive to live up to the professed tenure neutrality, the government deliberated about whether to end the provision of housing allowances to homeowners and to improve accessibility to these allowances by tenants in the formal private rental stock.

Financial Issues

State budget expenditures on housing have been gradually decreasing, reflecting the decentralization of housing policy to local levels. The government-funded programs have focused on several issues:

- Credit subsidies, such as interest buy-downs, to first-time home buyers of newly built dwellings (this is being phased out)
- Thermo-insulation loans for capital improvements of energy inefficient buildings
- Direct lending for construction of nonprofit rental buildings
- Construction of municipal social rental housing and infrastructure
- Lower value-added tax on building materials and moderate-cost housing.

Municipalities have been actively engaged in nonprofit TBS housing, in the financing and operation of local housing allowance schemes, and in the provision of general housing infrastructure.

Private Renting Activity

Private renting is quite active and serviced by licensed real estate brokers and property managers. Tenants come from the typical renting groups: young, mobile, and migrant, as well as those on low incomes. Those in "intermediate" households are shut off from the home ownership market on the one hand, and from social housing on the other hand. This activity is not well monitored as much of it is informal and untaxed. Brokers usually charge a half-month rent for finding tenants. If they also manage renting for the landlord, they take a percentage of gross rents—usually in the range 3–5 percent, and a security deposit of one month's rent. The deposit money is kept in a separate interest-bearing account. In cooperative and condominium dwellings rented individually, rents include utilities and partial furnishings. In "professional" rental buildings, utilities are paid separately and flats are typically unfurnished so that landlords receive net rental income with no risks related to utility costs. Both tenants and landlords in

the private rental sector have associations that help their members and participate in international federations.

Much of the private rental stock is old and in poor condition. Only those who
also have commercial premises are able to finance the necessary capital repairs
and renovation. There is very little commercial lending on these buildings
because of the various risks, insufficient tax incentives, and resultant low risk-
adjusted cash-flow performance. Tenants in these buildings are of varying socio-
economic status, reflecting past socialist administrative decisions about dwelling
allocation. Rent arrears in this segment are thought to be about 16 percent.

Private Rental Investment

Very little formal private investment has taken place in "professional" rental
apartment buildings. Investors seem to be waiting for the right conditions and
time. An individual investment in rental housing is often compared with an
investment in medium- and long-term government securities and analogous bank
term deposits. The net equity dividend ratio (that is, the ratio of net annual
income to price) in metropolitan cities has recently ranged from 4 to 5 percent;
the gross ratio is 4.5–5.5 percent. Inflation in Poland is about 3.8 percent. Net
interest (after-tax) rates on government securities (10 years) have ranged from
4.5 to 5 percent, and net interest rates (after-tax) on medium-term term deposits
(3 years) have ranged from 4 to 4.5 percent. Rental income from these investments is rarely reported for tax purposes. The profitability and pricing calculus
differs in the primary and secondary markets, mainly because the newly completed dwellings require additional finishing investments to make them
habitable.

One state bank is financing private rental investments using a project finance
approach. Some rental buildings are traded on the market, with prices sensitive
to risk factors such as tenant characteristics (age, arrears), and the existence of
additional commercial premises and the possibility of rooftop additions. Most of
these purchases are still based on equity financing. There is a growing debate on
the need to attract new categories of investors into the private rental segment.
There are calls for offering incentives to individual investors to become formally
registered taxpayer landlords. There is also discussion on how to create vehicles
through which passive individual investors could purchase participation in real
estate investment funds or trusts that would buy whole projects from
developers.

Social Renting Activities

Many of the remaining municipal rental units are dispersed in partially privatized
buildings with both tenant-owners and municipal tenants. In 80 percent of such
mixed-tenure buildings, tenant-owners have gained majority control and have
typically chosen private management companies. This has reduced the role of the
municipality to a passive member of the condominium association that sets
maintenance fees and renovation-fund contributions. These payments are often
higher than the regulated rent charged by the municipality to its tenants.

Municipalities retain the management of buildings that have no privatized flats or a minority of privatized flats. However, many municipalities liquidated housing management companies, often through employee buyouts, and opted for outsourcing to private companies including former municipal ones. By doing so, they were able to reduce subsidizing operation and maintenance costs, but they still face high costs for necessary capital repairs and renovation. Part of the social housing stock is also embodied in nonprofit TBS buildings, which balance their operations on rents not exceeding 4 percent of replacement cost. Housing allowances are used to help some households in this stock.

Much of the remaining municipal rental stock remains in poor condition. Rent arrears in this segment are rather high: 44 percent of tenants are late, and 15 percent of rental amounts due are not collected. This figure is only 4 percent in cooperatives. Additionally, because of the low rents, the turnover in this stock is minimal, which forces municipalities to look for alternative ways of providing social housing to those registered on waiting lists. The problem is exacerbated by the continued political pressure to privatize more of the stock to the sitting tenants. Consequently, municipalities are purchasing cooperative dwellings, converting nonresidential premises, and also using the TBS program. Some emergency and special-purpose housing is being built using another state funding program; it then must be subsidized to cover operation and maintenance costs. Some more innovative concepts being discussed include public-private partnership schemes to produce social rental housing supported by municipal guarantees and a closed investment fund focused on the development of social dwellings with cost-recovery rents. So far no practical example has been realized, but debates are lively and important in this area.

Russian Federation*

Like most other post-Soviet countries, the Russian Federation has viewed rental housing as a residual segment of housing policy. Consequently, most efforts have been directed at selling, if not giving away, units in multifamily buildings. The road toward home ownership has been long and protracted. Only recently have the policy makers acknowledged the need for a paradigm shift by recognizing the complementary role of rental housing. In particular, formalizing and institutionalizing informal or illegal renting by privatized former tenants appeared necessary as it has grown in response to the lack of formal renting tenure. The country has also recognized the need to create favorable conditions for market-based provisions of rental housing.

Housing Policy Framework
In Russia, the Ministry of Regional Development is responsible for housing policy. Since housing has been declared a national strategic issue, policy

*The Russian Federation case study was provided by Jan Brzeski.

formulation and implementation is overseen by the National Priority Project, "Comfortable and Affordable Housing for Russian Families." It operates as a permanent committee under the auspices of the president. Federally funded implementation programs are embodied in the Federal Target Program until 2020 and in several lesser programs for clean municipal water and for repair and modernization of the housing stock. Other housing-related programs at regional and local levels focus on specific issues. Local housing policies are rather weak because municipalities are not required to adopt specific local housing strategies to qualify for federal or regional housing-related support.

The legislative base consists primarily of the civil code, which sets a framework for residential renting activities and delegates more specific regulatory dispositions to the housing code, which focuses almost entirely on social housing activities. The main subsidy program on renting is embodied in housing allowances that help sitting municipal tenants and privatized tenant-owners pay housing and utility bills. There is no subsidy program targeted to tenants in the private rental segment. Recently, the government has embarked on an overhaul of the national housing policy and circulated a consultation paper "Current Problems of Socio-Economic Strategy of Russia till 2020 in the Area of Housing Policy."

Role of Rental Housing Sector in Housing Policy

During the two decades of transition since the collapse of the Soviet Union, the housing policy reform paradigm has been based on the goal of universal home ownership and thus was driven by universal microprivatization of municipal rental stock. The deadline for microprivatization has recently been extended to 2013.

Rental housing was seen as a residual of privatization and focused narrowly on social policy interventions. The present policy overhaul is signaling a considerable change in viewing rental housing's role as complementary instead of residual. Consequently, the government is showing growing interest in policy measures that foster tenure-neutral housing choice and thus imply a significant growth of the formal private rental housing sector. Furthermore, some policy makers acknowledge that private rental housing could well be a cheaper alternative to the heavily subsidized new construction of social housing, with the potential that the housing filtering process could produce a trickle-down of private housing stock to levels suitable for a social housing rental role.

Composition of the Housing Stock

A meaningful overview of the housing stock is difficult because housing policy debate and reporting continue to be based mostly on residential square footage rather than on dwelling numbers. The legal structure differs considerably from the occupancy structure, and comparisons are made even more difficult because of the high incidence of informal renting. Legally, home ownership lies at 75 percent and formal social rental housing at 25 percent. Functionally, however, some 65 percent of housing stock is owner occupied, 25 percent is rented in social housing stock owned by the state or municipality, and 8–10 percent is owned privately and rented informally. Additionally, many new dwellings are bought for speculative gains and are not occupied or rented, some of which have not been completed.

To make the situation even more complex, the majority of privatized flats are still on municipal balance sheets, as long as there are some nonprivatized municipal flats remaining there and as long as no homeowner association (HOA) has been formed to take over the responsibility. Whereas membership in HOAs remains voluntary, less than 10 percent of multifamily buildings have functioning HOAs. Because of the ambiguity over HOA formation and tenant-owner responsibility for maintaining common areas, the physical condition of multifamily buildings continues to deteriorate. That includes the stock of state and municipal dwellings slated for eventual privatization.

Rental Housing Sector

Only 20 percent of households can afford to improve their housing situation through mortgage-financed market purchases. Some 30 percent on lower incomes cannot make any move, and 50 percent of households on moderate incomes can neither access the "locked" social housing nor purchase their own dwelling.

Private Rental Housing

The private renting segment is estimated at 8–10 percent of the country's housing stock. There are no official statistics, because the overwhelming majority of these rentals are informal. Anecdotal evidence suggests that in Moscow some 17 percent of dwellings are tenant-occupied. The present overhaul of housing policy toward reviving the market-rented sector assumes that by 2020 formal private rental housing will have grown from 0 percent to between 5 and 7 percent of the total stock. Nonprofit and governmental rental housing will have grown from 0 percent to between 2 and 4 percent of the stock, while informal individual renting will retain its 8–10 percent share.

Private landlords consist mostly of individuals—typically privatized tenant-owners who have alternative accommodation—who want to supplement their income by renting informally to people who are shut out of either ownership or social housing segments: young, mobile and migrant, divorced and single, and newly poor and middle-income. Some renters are simply waiting for their parents, mostly privatized tenant-owners, to retire into suburban dachas. Wealthy, individual, buy-to-let investors are another visible category of landlords; their numbers grow when rents increase faster than prices. They are purchasing dwellings in primary and secondary markets to earn rental income (buy-to-let)—sometimes several apartments in one or in several buildings. Although intended to produce regular income, these investments are also seen as inflation and pension hedges and are expected to yield medium-term capital gains.

Social Rental Housing

Social rental stock, state and municipally owned, constitutes about 25 percent of the housing stock. Social rental housing, mostly municipal and some state, is viewed as housing that has not yet been privatized. Because municipalities are usually financially strapped and believe they will eventually lose this stock, the buildings continue to deteriorate, which might discourage sitting tenants from privatizing for fear of excessive renovation costs. Policy makers expect this market rental housing, both for-profit and nonprofit, to increase its share, which will lead to a reduction in the share of social rental housing stock from 25 percent today to 13 percent in 2020. No form of rental housing other than state and municipal forms has been developed under nonprofit cost-coverage principles.

Rental Housing Regulatory Framework

The general relationship for residential renting is regulated in the civil code (chapter 35), which delegates social renting regulations to the housing code that includes the housing allowance scheme. There is no specific regulatory act on the tenant–landlord relationship for private renting.

Private Renting

Because chapter 35 of the civil code provides only general directions, numerous aspects of the rental relationship are regulated in rental contracts, whether verbal or written. For example, there are no specific civil code regulations on eviction issues and dispute resolution procedures. Rental contracts, if in writing, are almost always for a period under one year to avoid being classified as social rental under the purview of the housing code, with restrictive eviction rights (for example, a required six months of arrears). Such written short-term contracts are not notarized or registered and are used mostly when rental brokers are involved to secure payment of their brokerage commission. Because of the lack of detailed contracting regulations, brokers often step in with contracting advice and sometimes with arbitration of disputes. The government has been trying to encourage informal landlords to come into the open, but with little to no success.

Social Renting

Social renting is limited to residual municipal stock, most of which probably will be privatized eventually by sitting tenants. However, some of the newly acquired stock is to be shielded from privatization claims. A new era for social housing will dawn once the privatization is final in 2013. Most of tenants' payments go to maintenance fees, utility bills, and sometimes "pure rent" if municipalities decide to charge it. Maintenance fees are low: they cover only current maintenance and do not charge for capital repairs, including funding for the future, because it is often implicitly assumed that tenants and tenant-owners are not responsible for common areas. Pure rent, if charged, is usually 1–2 percent of the maintenance fee and does not reflect profit to the landlord or land rent. Utility bills are very high relative to maintenance and rent. As a rule, they are set at about 90 percent of cost-recovery levels, which are high because of inefficiencies such as poor insulation, plumbing leaks, and inefficient employment structures and processes. The housing code confers an indefinite term on the social rental agreement, irrespective of changes in the financial status of social tenants, thus creating strong disincentives for moving and relinquishing the allocated dwelling.

Taxation Regulations

Individual landlords who have decided to move into the formal sector, can register under one of two personal income-tax regimes for taxing their rental activities: (a) regular PIT or (b) simplified tax for individual entrepreneurs and the self employed. The PIT regime is viewed as very complicated and as requiring frequent visits to tax offices. Finding out what expenses incurred to earn rental income are allowed to lower landlords' taxable income is difficult. A flat PIT rate of 13 percent is applied to this income. The simplified tax regime is viewed as more advantageous to individual landlords. It can be used in two ways: (a) gross flat rate of 6 percent without any deductions or (b) net rate of 15 percent applied after making deductions. The simplified regime requires quarterly declarations. Neither regime allows deductions for capital depreciation or has provisions for loss carry-forward.

Financial Issues

There is virtually no specialized market lending to buy-to-let investments, so there are no guarantees and subsidies either. The very few social housing investments are budget financed. Given that most activities in the private rental sector are informal, there is no rental insurance either.

Private Renting Activity

Private-rental sector activity is not monitored officially at any government level, so reliable data are lacking; anecdotal evidence is fragmented and based on individual episodes. The most accurate knowledge of this market segment is held by rental brokers and managers, who service a considerable share of the market. Anecdotal evidence from Moscow suggests that brokers handle up to 70 percent of private renting, whereas 30 percent is done by individual landlords. The brokers and managers typically are hired by a variety of owners:

- Younger people who inherited a dwelling and live somewhere else
- Individual "amateur" buy-to-let investors
- Absentee investors holding dwellings for future use
- Residents of suburban dachas who own a dwelling in the city
- Those who move from the city during the warm season, renting to students for four to five months.

Rental contracts typically include heating and furnishings. Demand for rental dwellings is about three times the supply in Moscow, so this is a landlords' market.

Hence, the brokers take their commission from tenants, not from landlords. The commission is between 50 and 100 percent of the monthly rent. There is also a security deposit equivalent to one month's rent. Most rental contracts are for less than one year.

Private Rental Investment

Private buy-to-let investments in dwellings are often compared with investment in medium- and long-term government securities and analogous bank term deposits. Rental income is typically not reported for tax purposes, and the profitability and pricing calculus differs between the primary and secondary markets. Dwellings in the secondary market are fully finished and carry relatively low operating and maintenance expenses because they are typically subsidized by the municipal companies that still manage these buildings. This will change when the ongoing drive to privatize building management companies is implemented in a few years. Dwellings in the primary market require additional outlays for finishing. This is often 30 percent or more of the purchase price. Their operating and maintenance expenses are high because there are no subsidies for managing new buildings. Property taxes are not significant, but after 2013, when ad valorem property tax is expected to be implemented, they may increase considerably for high-value properties.

The present yield levels have been ranging around 6–7 percent on net rents (annual net rent and acquisition cost) and 7–8 percent on gross rents. These are yields in Moscow, which is the main market for buy-to-let investors. In another city, Ryazan, a similar calculation reveals a ratio of about 6 percent. These are informal, rough estimates because transaction prices are not reported and only listing prices are used in property valuations. This ratio is typically compared with interest rates on government securities and bank term-deposit rates, even though their cash-flow and risk profiles are different. Medium-term rates on government securities and bank deposits range from 8 to 10 percent, although they do not offer capital gains potential. Reportedly, given these levels, some investor interest has been returning to the buy-to-let segment. Currently, bank credit costs about 12 percent while inflation is at 9.5 percent.

Attracting corporate investors to buy newly built buildings from developers is still not considered an interesting proposition, because developers think they are better off selling their buildings piecemeal to individual investors who then rent their dwelling informally and skip paying taxes. Nevertheless, some attempts are occasionally being undertaken to "test the market." In two cases anecdotally mentioned in Moscow, (a) a state company has built one "experimental" rental building and (b) several businesspeople formed a joint venture for investing their formal profits into a formal residential rental building, hired a developer to build it, and then contracted a property management company to generate rental income. Some other renting businesses, especially in St. Petersburg, are reportedly run as "apart-hotels," which mimic private rental operations.

Housing Allowances

Means-tested housing allowances have been used in Russia for many years but applied only to municipal tenants and privatized tenant-owners. Private renting tenants can theoretically apply for them. But first they would need to have formal contracts. Then their rent would be calibrated to the social rental sector, which has drastically lower rents than what they actually pay in private rental, so the allowance is unlikely to be awarded. The current lack of applicability of the housing allowance system to private rentals (actual rents) makes this segment of housing stock unavailable to vulnerable households. Those vulnerable households continue to swell waiting lists for the shrinking social stock. Moscow is considering encouraging private renting by reducing subsidies for purchasing dwellings and introducing housing allowances for tenants in private rented housing—not least to encourage the formalization of private rental contracts.

Social Renting Activities

Social renting activities are governed by the housing code, while the stock is treated as a temporary residual of microprivatization. Rents continue to be grossly insufficient, and the government is trying to relieve local governments of excessive subsidies for operation and maintenance given to the occupiers of this stock by mandating the privatization of municipal housing management companies and the introduction of market-priced building management. This would introduce cost-recovery principles and thus reduce subsidies for operation and maintenance services while leaving capital repairs an unresolved issue. The government hopes to develop a more rational social housing system once the microprivatization program is over, possibly by 2013.

Singapore*

Singapore is a densely populated city-state with an area of 712 square kilometers and a population of 5.07 million, of which 3.77 million are residents.[11] Over the past six decades, Singapore has built an impressive stock of housing through heavy state involvement.

When self-government began in 1959, deplorable housing conditions and housing shortages were exacerbated by rapid postwar growth. The People's Action Party government made housing a priority area of policy concern. Housing institutions and policies were developed systematically and comprehensively to advance social development and economic growth (Phang 2007, 19).

The Housing and Development Board (HDB) established in 1960, with an initial mandate to provide basic rental accommodation for the poor, was a key institution. Since the Home Ownership Scheme (HOS) was introduced in 1964, home ownership has been promoted as an integral part of nation building. Through HOS, eligible households could purchase a 99-year leasehold interest in their flat, but not in the land or common areas, at a subsidized price. These units

---

*The Singapore case study was provided by Kyung-Hwan Kim.

were initially sold at a discount but could be traded in the open resale market after the flats had been occupied for a minimum of five years. HDB has built about 1 million residential units over the past 50 years. By 1990, the ratio of the number of housing units to that of resident households reached 104 percent.

Description of the Rental Sector

In this section, we describe the distribution of housing tenure, the stock of rental dwellings available, the quality of rental housing, and the rent burden.

Distribution of Housing Tenure

Housing tenure forms are quite complex. In fact, public–private hybrids are sometimes defined as owned units, as rental units, as HDB, or as private units. Land ownership is defined by freehold, state-owned leasehold (and number of years of remaining leasehold), fully owned, or part owned status. Singapore is unique in that the vast majority of its residents live in dwellings built by the public sector and the public housing stock is predominantly owner occupied. The resident home ownership rate was 87.2 percent in 2010, lower than the 92.0 percent of 2000 but still among the highest in the world. As of 2010, 82 percent of the resident population lives in HDB flats, including 79 percent in owner-occupied flats. The total housing stock in 2010 was 1,180,500 units, of which HDB holds 898,500. The remaining 258,200 are owned by the private sector.[12] Other key indicators appear in table 5.7.

The Stock of Rental Housing

Rental housing represents a very small portion of the housing stock. In the public sector, 95 percent of HDB units are for owner occupation. Rental units represent

Table 5.7 Singapore: Key Housing Sector Indicators

	1970	1980	1990	2000	2010
Population ('000)	207.5	241.4	304.7	402.8	507.7
Resident population	201.4	228.2	273.6	327.3	377.2
Nonresident population	61	132	311	757	1,305
Resident households ('000)	380.5	509.5	661.7	915.1	1,345.9
Resident home ownership rate (%)	29	59	88	92	87.2
Resident population in HDB units (%)	36	73	87	87.7	82.4
Per capita GNI (S$)	2,825	9,941	22,645	42,212	57,603
Gross fixed capital formation/GDP (%)	32.2	42.2	31.6	27.6	25
Housing investment/GDP (%)	6.2	5.9	5.2	6.2	6.8
Housing stock ('000)	305.8	467.1	690.6	1,046.2	1,180.5
Public sector built	120.1	337.2	574.4	846.7	898.5
Private sector built	185.7	129.9	116.1	193	258.2
Dwelling units per 1,000 persons	147	194	227	259	233
Dwelling units per 1,000 residents	152	205	252	319	313
Housing stock/resident households	80.4	91.7	104.4	112.6	103

Sources: Phang 2005; Department of Statistics of Singapore.
Note: GDP = gross domestic product; GNI = gross national product; HDB = Housing and Development Board.

only 5 percent of the public housing stock. HDB flats can be rented to tenants who are citizens or permanent residents. The private rental market operates freely and serves the needs of expatriates. Rent control, which was first implemented in 1947 by the British colonial government, was lifted in 2001.

Quality of Rental Housing and the Burden of Rents

The rental housing sector is divided into the regulated rental sector and the unregulated private rental sector. In HDB sublet housing, units that have been privately owned and occupied for five years can be leased to citizens and permanent residents with prior approval from HDB at market-determined rents. This subsector has been enlarged significantly since 2003, with changes to HDB's subletting rules (Lum 2011). HDB social rental housing comprises smaller, low-cost rental units provided directly by HDB for low-income households. This represents the social housing sector for Singaporeans, especially since rent control in the private housing sector was phased out. A proportion of HDB's rental units also cater to transitional families—those waiting for their Home Ownership flat—as well as to foreign workers. The private rental stock consists of high-quality dwellings to serve foreigners and locals with high income. Rents are determined completely by market forces.

The Legal Framework

This section provides a brief description of the legal framework within which the rental sector operates, focusing on tenant protection and taxation.

Tenant Protection

There are no tenant protection laws. The terms of rental lease are negotiated in the contract. The tenant is supposed to make a security deposit equivalent to one month's rent. The deposit is refunded without interest at the expiration of termination of the lease. In addition to the deposit, one month's rent is prepaid. The lease period is generally at least one year and can be extended by mutual agreement.

Taxation

Property tax is levied on immovable properties, including all houses, land, buildings, and tenements. The tax is levied on the annual value of the property at a rate of 4 percent per year of one owner-occupied residential property and 10 percent for other properties. The annual value of residential properties is the gross amount at which the property can reasonably be expected to be let from year to year, with the landlord paying the expenses of repair, insurance, maintenance or upkeep, and all taxes other than GST (goods and services tax). The estimated annual value of property is thought to be between 80 and 90 percent of annual market rent.

The stamp duty is a tax on executed documents relating to the acquisition, disposal, and leases of properties. Stamp duty on rental leases, involving a fixed rental throughout the rental period, is computed based on the gross rent. Stamp duty on leases is computed on all charges (except GST) paid by the tenant to the landlord. The rate is S$1 for every S$250 or part thereof on the average annual rent for a one-year lease, S$2 for a one- to three-year lease, and S$4 for leases exceeding three years.

Rental income is subjected to income taxation. The taxable income is computed by deducting property tax, insurance, and maintenance and repair expenses from the gross rental income. Depreciation allowance is not deductible. There is no capital gains tax.

Financial Issues

Concessionary loans and subsidies play a significant role in the rental housing sector. Table 5.8 summarizes the annual rate of increase in the housing price and rent series as well as that of the consumer price index since 1990. It shows that the average rate of change was larger for the asset price of housing than for rents but that rents have been much more volatile than housing prices, as shown in figure 5.5.

Table 5.8 Singapore: Annual Average Rate of Change in Housing Prices and Rents

Year	RPPI	HDB resale price index	Rental index	CPI
1990	13.2	—	—	3.5
1991	10.4	2.4	17.4	3.4
1992	15.8	9.0	8.7	2.3
1993	27.6	50.8	3.4	2.3
1994	43.6	30.9	−3.5	3.1
1995	17.6	23.9	2.2	1.7
1996	11.5	39.9	2.3	1.4
1997	−8.7	3.9	−8.5	2.0
1998	−26.5	−18.6	−17.0	−0.3
1999	5.2	−1.5	−15.4	0.0
2000	14.1	4.2	3.6	1.3
2001	−10.0	−8.8	−2.4	1.0
2002	−6.4	−2.6	−2.7	−0.4
2003	−1.8	5.3	−4.2	0.5
2004	−0.3	4.1	−1.4	1.7
2005	2.9	−2.5	2.6	0.5
2006	7.1	0.0	7.8	1.0
2007	23.4	9.4	33.3	2.1
2008	13.4	19.1	21.4	6.6
2009	−13.8	7.4	−16.2	0.6
2010	25.9	14.2	10.1	2.8
Mean	7.8	9.5	2.1	1.8
Standard deviation	16.0	16.5	12.5	1.6
Standard deviation/mean	2.1	1.7	6.0	0.9

Sources: RPPI, HDB resale price index, rental index, and CPI data.
Note: — = not available; CPI = Consumer Price Index; HDB = Housing and Development Board; RPPI = Retail Property Price Index.

Figure 5.5 Singapore: Rate of Change in Housing Prices and Rents

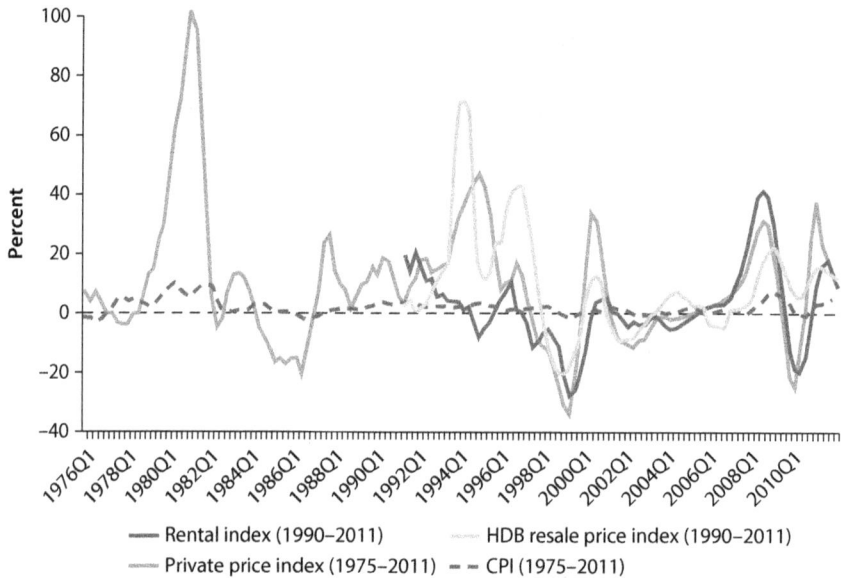

Note: CPI = Consumer Price Index; HDB = Housing and Development Board.

Loans

HDB flat purchases are financed through concessionary loans from HDB, mortgages from financial institutions at market rates, as well as withdrawal of savings in the Central Provident Fund (CPF) and additional CPF housing grants. CPF savings could be used to pay up to 100 percent of the valuation or purchase price of the HDB flat, whichever was lower, or to fund the down payment and transaction costs, with the balance of the purchase price financed by an HDB loan. For the most part, the contract interest rate on HDB loans was tied to the CPF savings rate and was below the housing loan rate charged by commercial banks. Households that were ineligible for HDB concessionary loans could obtain market-rate loans from the HDB for buying public housing or from private players. The HDB mortgage market was liberalized in 2003, when HDB ceased to provide market-rate loans to flat buyers and concessionary loans were subjected to the same CPF rulings as private sector loans.

International banks are the main supplier of mortgage loans in the private sector. Over time, adjustable-rate mortgages with up-front teaser rates and longer repayment periods (of up to 35 years) have become prevalent. Lenders typically priced floating-rate loans against either the Singapore Interbank Offered Rate (SIBOR) or the prime rate. A market for securitization does not exist.

Subsidized Public Rental Housing

The HDB rental stock provides subsidized basic housing for low-income households. One- or two-bedroom HDB flats are rented at heavily subsidized rents to citizens whose household income is S$1,500 or less per month and who have no other housing options or family support. Rents are tiered, depending on income level as well as whether the household has received a housing subsidy before. Households in the income range of S$801–1,500 pay monthly rents pegged at 30 percent of the market rent. For households with incomes not exceeding S$800, the monthly rent is about 10 percent of the market rate. The basic rent can be as low as S$30 for a one-room rental flat, if the household income is S$800 or less and it has not received housing subsidies before. These rental units are available for two years and can be renewed.

Support to Private Rental Housing Production

Private developers play a limited role of supplying expensive dwellings to the higher-income groups as well as expatriates and foreign investors. The vast majority of residents live in public housing. No financial incentives are available for the production of private rental housing. Real estate investment trusts and institutional investors are not involved in the private rental housing business. A main reason is that the gross yield (without considering vacancy and other costs) on rental housing is very low. According to the *Global Property Guide*, the gross yield ranged from 2.2 to 3.3 percent as of June 2010. This is compared to a bond yield of 1.4 percent at the same time.

Direct Subsidies to Tenants

Although subsidies for home purchases have moved from supply-side subsidies to demand-side subsidies over the years, there are no direct subsidies to tenants.

Conclusion

Singapore has promoted home ownership through various policies since 1964, and its current home ownership rate is among the highest in the world. However, the small public rental housing sector serves the housing needs of low-income households. The private rental sector operates freely to cater to the demand by residents as well as foreigners.

Thailand*

The rental housing market in Thailand—and in Bangkok, in particular—is multifaceted. It serves many groups with different products and several sources of financing. Some experts have argued that it is an efficient market, with little or no need for governmental intervention. Others note that there are still a great many people in need, particularly those who live in slums or in squatter settlements.

The private sector is actively involved in providing rental housing, particularly for lower-income workers and for students. It is a market dominated by small landlords; some who own what can be termed "self-help housing," that is, a room in their own house or an apartment in the same building in which the landlord lives. Those who own multiple units are still small landlords. In one study, landlords owned an average of 39 units; none owned more than 100.

---

*The Thailand case study was provided by Ira Peppercorn.

In the public sector, the government created three housing-related organizations, all of which play some role in rental housing development and finance. The Government Housing Bank (GH Bank), the nation's largest provider of affordable mortgages, also finances developers of rental housing. The National Housing Authority (NHA) develops housing projects, some of which have been used for rental. The Community Organizations Development Institute (CODI) handles the most difficult challenges of slums and squatter settlements. Its practices, although not truly rental housing, are alternatives to home ownership.

Although these institutions provide much of what is needed in the rental-housing sector, more still needs to be done. The government's housing organizations note that a national housing policy needs to be formally adopted and that rental housing and other types of non-ownership models should play a strong role in this policy. The fact that more than 4 million people live in units built from nonpermanent materials shows that housing conditions need to be improved.

Demographics

According to the 2000 census, Thailand had a population of nearly 61 million people, making it the fourth-largest country in Southeast Asia in population. Indonesia had the largest population (209 million), followed by Vietnam (79 million) and the Philippines (74 million).

In 2000, there were nearly 16 million households in Thailand. The average size had shrunk to 3.9 persons per household from the 1990 figure of 4.4. Approximately one-third of the population lives in a metropolitan area. There were 6,320,174 people in Bangkok (10.4 percent of the population). Current estimates are that Bangkok has grown even further and now has approximately 10 million residents.

In a trend toward urbanization, the number of people working in the agriculture sector declined from 67 percent of the population to 56 percent between 1990 and 2000. Those considered employees increased to 36 percent from 27 percent in the same time period, while unpaid family workers declined by almost the same amount.

As Thailand urbanizes, one notable trend is that the percentage of Thai families owning a home is declining—from 87 percent in 1990 to 82 percent in 2000. This is primarily because of an increase in tenancy in urban areas as can be seen in table 5.9.

Table 5.9 Thailand: Housing Characteristics, National and Bangkok

Housing characteristics	Thailand	Bangkok
Private households ('000)	15,877	1,740
Average household size (persons)	3.8	3.6
Houses of nonpermanent materials (%)	7.1	4.2
Households with ownership (%)	82.4	55.6
Households with sanitation (%)	97.8	99.8

Source: National Statistics Office, Thailand, 2000.

Table 5.10 Thailand: Main Residence by Tenure

Type of housing	Total		Municipal area		Nonmunicipal area	
	Households	Share (%)	Households	Share (%)	Households	Share (%)
Owner occupied	12,512,708	78.8	3,129,390	59.6	9,383,316	88.3
Hired purchaser	261,209	1.6	164,172	3.1	97,040	0.9
Rental	1,673,639	10.5	1,358,290	25.9	315,352	3.0
Housing in kind for service	260,632	1.6	141,679	2.7	118,953	1.1
Rent free	792,936	5.0	351,235	6.7	441,698	4.2
Unknown	376,074	2.4	109,033	2.1	267,034	2.5

Source: National Statistics Office, Thailand, 2000.

Households living in units made of nonpermanent materials can be used as a gauge for those living in slums or in squatter settlements. While the national trend decreased from 9.4 to 7.1 percent, the percentage of those living in substandard housing actually rose by 75 percent in Bangkok, from 2.4 to 4.2 percent.

In Bangkok, the percentage of those owning homes declined from 61.1 to 55.6 percent between 1990 and 2000. Some assume from this that the percentage of renters is 44.4 percent; in reality, only a portion of those who do not own homes are renters. They might be living in quarters in exchange for work, or living rent free, or in some other type of arrangement that is not defined. This distinction is critical because those who are neither owners nor renters are the most likely to be living as squatters or slum dwellers.

Those formally classified as renters are far more likely to live in cities than in nonmetropolitan areas (25.9 percent compared with 3 percent). City dwellers are far less likely to live in a detached unit than those dwelling outside urban areas (50.8 versus 91 percent) and more likely to live in a row house, a town house, or an apartment, which is reflected in table 5.10.

Given these factors, what do we know about the rental market in Thailand and about the conditions in which people live?

Studies of Bangkok

One of the only recent studies on rental housing in Thailand (Perera 2005) looked at six districts within the Bangkok metropolitan region. It focused on private rental housing occupied by low-income households and students residing in formal, multistory rental units and houses. It did not include those living in rental housing provided by the government, institutional housing provided by employers, or land rental slums or those squatting in informal settlements.

Perera (2005, 9) made the following observations about tenants:

- Tenants were most likely to be young workers in factories, services workers, those employed by small business or informal businesses, young factory workers, simple wagerworkers, small-business enterprisers, private workers, and students.

- Proximity to the workplace and the availability of rental housing units were the two considerations for working tenants to move to their current location.
- Only 45 percent of tenants had a written agreement with the landlord.
- The majority of the tenants had resided for less than two years in their last rental unit and had been living for less than five years in the present one. This was because they change the location of their workplace often.
- The tenants who were interviewed preferred to rent for the time being because it suited them. This was true not only for students but also for factory workers.
- The tenants studied did not spend a high proportion of their income on rent. One study noted that the range was from 10 to 20 percent.

One interesting finding was that one-third of the tenants interviewed owned property outside the Bangkok metropolitan region. It was their intent to stay in the city only temporarily. They hoped to go back to their home region. "About 85 percent of the tenants residing in private sector rental housing preferred home ownership ... a significant proportion of tenants intended to go back to their hometown" (Perera 2005, 9).

As for the landlords:

- On average, small landlords owned between four and 40 units. The landlords split into two groups: those who owned only one rental unit and those who owned multiple properties, which did not exceed 100 in this study.
- The majority of the landlords studied that operated on a small scale owned about one rental property. "They are rather like their tenants, do not make much money" (Perera 2005, 10).
- The smaller landlords were likely to live in the same community—or even in the same building—as their tenants.
- Landlords preferred to keep tenants' tenure informal and did not generally have written leases.
- These landlords often avoided paying taxes on the rental income.
- Although this study did not mention expected rates of return for the landlord, small owners interviewed for this book stated that they anticipated an 8 to 10 percent pretax return.[13]
- Interviews with rental housing owners also noted that, in cases of nonpayment, they were not concerned about legal processes or about the time it would take to evict a tenant, as landlords in other countries were.
- The finding that most landlords are similar in income and status to their tenants has been seen in other studies as well. A United Nations report on housing states, "Since most landlords are little better off than their tenants, support for rental housing is not an inequitable policy. Indeed, encouraging self-help landlords to construct for rent generally helps them to improve the housing stock, creates more space, and improves the vitality of low-income suburbs" (UN-HABITAT 2003).

Based on the results of his survey, Perera noted, "the rental housing for the lower-income by landlords in Bangkok demonstrated a market-driven supply of affordable rental units based on increasing demand without government intervention or subsidies to either the landlord or the urban poor" (2005, 11). Although this might indeed be true for that segment of the population that Perera interviewed for his study, it did not address those living in government-provided housing, in slums, or in squatters' settlements. Moreover, other studies came to different conclusions. Another study noted that "low-income households in Bangkok have traditionally resorted to renting vacant land where they construct informal slum housing. This is because there is a lack of affordable formal housing" (Yap 1996).

The Government's Approach

The government divides its housing functions among three organizations:

- GH Bank provides loans to developers of multifamily rental housing.
- NHA, a state enterprise under the Ministry of Social Development and Human Security, develops and manages housing, partners with private developers, and provides subsidies for those seeking affordable housing. It has built and managed rental housing.
- CODI, the former governmental Urban Community Development Office, works with local community organizations to develop solutions for squatters and slum dwellers. Although its housing solutions under the Baan Mankong Program are not technically rental, they are an alternative to home ownership.

Interviews with officials from these organizations demonstrated that all believe rental housing should be an important part of the government's priorities. Each of these organizations has its own role, with GH Bank providing financing, NHA acting as a developer and provider of subsidies, and CODI targeting integrated community-based solutions. They also serve different populations, with CODI generally handling the poorest, NHA handling low-income people, and GH Bank serving a broad range of customers.

GH Bank

The Ministry of Finance owns GH Bank, which was chartered in 1953. It was originally both a financier and a developer. However, in 1973, the development role was split off when the government created the NHA and moved the housing development activities to that agency. GH Bank now focuses solely on financing activities.

GH Bank's main role is as a direct mortgage lender. It is more than a financier of single-family mortgages. To stimulate the economy and provide financing for the development of affordable housing, GH Bank also provides financing to developers for rental housing. Under the board of investment's housing investment policy, developers can apply for project financing for rental projects that (a) have a minimum of 50 units that do not exceed 28 square meters and

(b) are targeted for affordable housing. According to the staff at GH Bank, this financing is highly competitive: the term can extend to 15 years and the developer can receive an income-tax exemption for 5–8 years.

Surachai Fangchanda, vice president of GH Bank, notes that the bank changed its strategy after 2006 to encourage smaller-scale rental developments, which fit more closely with Thailand's culture and which historically have been more successful. In 2006, the average number of units built per loan originated was 1,129; in 2009, it was 312.

Interviews with developers show both the risk and the opportunities in this strategy. On the one hand, it relies on the resources of private developers and does so with a minimum of bureaucracy. On the other hand, these units will generally not be for the very poor. That function has been shifted primarily to CODI. Additionally, although many of the developers have the financial wherewithal to build a 100-unit project, it is unclear whether they have the requisite capital to manage the projects in the event of a major economic downturn. In either case, the number of units being financed under this program is relatively small.

National Housing Authority

NHA's role in the provision of rental housing is as a developer, manager, owner, and provider of subsidies. Between 1976 and 2008, NHA constructed or reha-bilitated 641,918 units. Of these, 289,254 (45 percent) were related to slum upgrading and 154,584 (24 percent) were built under the Baan Eua Arthorn (low-cost housing) program. Approximately 16,000 units were built for rental housing.

NHA grants subsidies of B 80,000 for the purpose of home purchase. It also permits the subsidies to be used in the development of rental housing, provided that the total unit cost is not more than approximately B 390,000.

In 2004, the government pledged to construct 1 million new homes. NHA would handle new construction and major rehabilitation, which was estimated to cover 600,000 units, a portion of which would be for rental. CODI would handle slum upgrading. Unfortunately, NHA incurred large losses on its development projects, particularly those under the Baan Eua Arthorn program. NHA officials are now seeking new roles and types of practices, such as partnering with developers in creating rental housing.

Community Development Organizations Institute (CODI)

In an effort to eradicate slums and to provide a better living standard for squat-ters, CODI takes a broad community development strategy in which its housing is neither home ownership nor rental. Rather, it is an integrated, community-based strategy that is based on a type of cooperative model.

CODI estimates that the number of people living in substandard housing is significant: 8.25 million in 5,500 communities; 65 percent of them on rented land with no secure contract; and 35 percent as squatters. Three-quarters of these residents cannot afford a home, and approximately 8 percent face the threat of eviction.

Table 5.11 Thailand: Use of Subsidies

Use	Amount (B)	Share (%)
Infrastructure	45,000	64
Land cost and housing subsidy	20,000	28
Administrative subsidy	700	1
Process support subsidy	5,000	7

Source: CODI 2009a.

Table 5.12 Thailand: CODI Ownership Structures

Structure	Number	Share (%)
Cooperative land ownership	23,479	44
Long-term lease to community cooperative	20,980	39
Short-term lease (fewer than five years) to community cooperative	4,143	8

Source: CODI 2009b.

CODI works with communities to gain secure title for the underlying land. It then uses a combination of its funds, governmental subsidies, and residents' funds to build or fix the infrastructure and, subsequently, to build the housing. CODI's 2008 report notes that it has assisted 54,000 households in 1,010 communities. More recent estimates are that this number is now approximately 77,000. Tables 5.11 and 5.12 show CODI's use of subsidies and the types of ownership structures that they use.

Conclusion

The responsibility for the development and financing of rental housing resides in a number of entities. Both the public and private sectors are involved with relatively clearly defined roles and in a way that matches the segmentation of the market itself. The market appears to work efficiently on the upper and middle ends. Even on the lower end, some argue that rental housing is affordable and that it meets the needs of the consumers. However, the greatest need is in the lower end of the market, particularly for those living in slums and in squatters' settlements. Here the limitations of the nation's housing policies can be seen. Although there have been positive efforts to resolve this difficult problem, not enough resources have been dedicated to its resolution.

United States*

There is a common perception that the United States is a nation of homeowners and that its federal policies reflect this priority. In the wake of the mortgage crisis, the challenges of ownership are becoming clearer. When housing prices are rising, those who do not buy a home can easily be shut out of the housing

---

*The United States case study was provided by Ira Peppercorn.

market. Often, once a house is purchased, the owner has the potential to have more equity than would otherwise be possible. However, when housing prices are falling—as is the case in many countries, including the United States—an owner can lose not only the equity in the house, but the house itself through default and foreclosure.

While many have indeed benefited financially from home ownership, recent studies indicate that the numbers might have been smaller than believed. A recent study noted that the financial gains of home ownership occurred only about half the time compared with renting and investing. It argues that a more balanced view of "the relative advantages and disadvantages of home ownership could have important macroeconomic implications" (Rappaport 2010, 53).

The *New York Times* reported that "Housing prices are now back to where they were in mid-2002 even before taking inflation into account. Such a decline was unimaginable to the boosters and many of the analysts in the middle of the boom, who were fond of saying that house prices never fell on a national basis. But as credit dried up and the easy refinances disappeared, the foreclosures began. Prices fell sharply in late 2006, 2007, and 2008" (Streitfeld 2011).

The percentage of the U.S. population who are homeowners has fallen from a peak of more than 69 percent to just over 66 percent, the ownership rate more than 20 years ago, according to the U.S. Census Bureau (figure 5.6).

The disparity in income levels between those who own and those who rent is significant. Families with incomes above the median income have an ownership rate of 80.8 percent; those with incomes below the median have only a 51.3 percent rate. The divide splits along racial and ethnic lines as well.

Figure 5.6 United States: Home Ownership Rate, 1965–2010

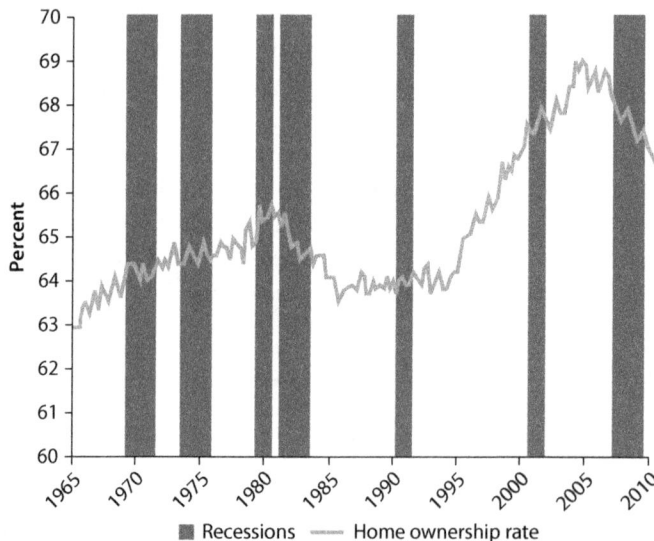

Source: U.S. Census Bureau.
Note: Share of occupied homes that are owner-occupied. Not seasonally adjusted.

The home ownership rate is 73.7 percent for white families. African American families have a rate of 45.1 percent and Latino families have a rate of 46.6 percent.

The implications are clear: there are times when rental is the only option and there are times when it is a choice. The mortgage crisis caused pressure on the rental market. Foreclosures skyrocketed and families that were owners and that lost their homes had to rent. Mortgage underwriters put in much stricter credit standards for loans, closing out a segment of the market that might have been able to qualify before. Other families chose not to buy a home because of fears that the real estate market in which they lived would continue to decline. As an executive of Toll Brothers, a luxury home building company noted, more people are choosing to rent rather than own. "There's no question that people are reticent to own. They're renting, and they're happy renting because they're scared."[14]

Right after the mortgage crisis, in 2008, the median rent was US$712—just below the historic highs. It has been increasing steadily since 1995, when the median rent was under US$450 (figure 5.7). Nor is it a surprise that vacancy rates have been decreasing. The vacancy rate for rental housing was 9.4 percent as of the fourth quarter of 2011, down from a high of 11.1 percent in the third quarter of 2009 and the lowest since 2003.

Meanwhile, the number of families seeking rental has increased. From 2006 to 2010, the number of renter households jumped by 692,000 a year, on average, to 37 million. The number of owner households fell on net by 201,000.

The rent burden continues to increase. The U.S. Census Bureau defines a rent burden as when a family must pay more than 35 percent of its gross rent on housing. In 2011, more than two in five renters (42.3 percent) were considered rent burdened, and 26 percent spent more than half of their income

Figure 5.7 United States: Rental Rates per Month, 1995–2011

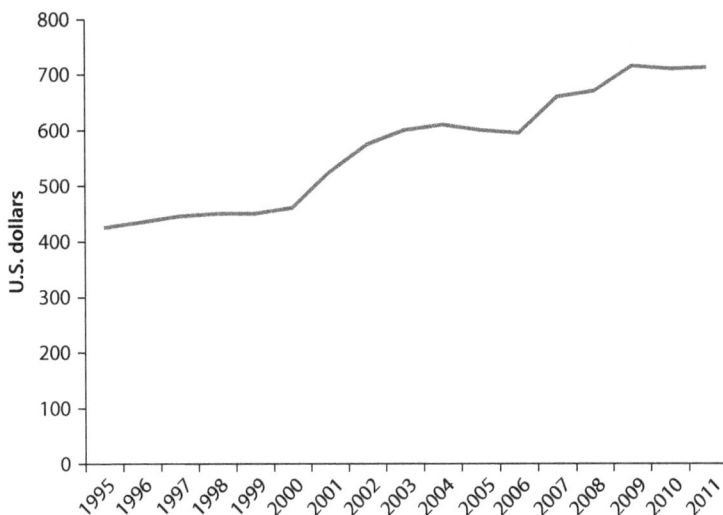

Source: U.S. Bureau of the Census, American Community Survey, 2012.

Rental Housing • http://dx.doi.org/10.1596/978-0-8213-9655-1

on rent (ElBoghdady 2011). There is a great disparity in the rental burden from city to city. In the Florida region consisting of Miami, Ft. Lauderdale, and Pompano Beach, an area that experienced one of the highest foreclosure rates in the nation, 54.3 percent of rental households were considered burdened.

There is a key significance in the difference between the percentage of income paid by homeowners and that paid by renters. Homeowners can deduct mortgage interest from their income taxes. In the early years of ownership, that interest constitutes nearly all of the mortgage payment. Renters, by contrast, cannot deduct their rental payments, although some states permit a small deduction.

The mortgage crisis was not the only reason for the tightening of rental markets. From 1995 to 2005, two rental units were permanently removed from the supply for every three produced. Over this same period, the nation permanently lost 1.5 million low-cost rental units. According to the U.S. census, only 124,000 properties with two or more units were built in 2010, the lowest level in nearly two decades.

From 2001 to 2007, the nation's stock of affordable unassisted rental housing decreased by 6.3 percent, while the high-rent rental housing stock increased 94.3 percent. This translates into a loss of more than 1.2 million affordable unassisted rental units from 2001 to 2007.

Types of Properties and Owners

Despite the common myth that most apartments in the United States are owned by large organizations, the reality is quite different. More than half of the apartments are in buildings that have between one and four units. More than one-third of the rental units are in single-family homes. The figure has been increasing since the mortgage crisis caused millions of mortgage borrowers to default. Individuals and couples owned more than 85 percent of small properties.

Thirty percent of all rentals are in properties with more than 50 units. Corporations and private partnerships own the vast majority of large multifamily properties (Joint Center for Housing Studies 2009). Mid-size multifamily properties of between 5 and 49 units constitute approximately 20 percent of the rental stock.

The reasons for owning multifamily properties vary with the number of properties owned and the type of owner. All multifamily owners want the cash flow that derives from rent. Beyond that, owners of small properties want a way to offset housing costs or to build an asset for retirement. Owners of large properties were far more likely to be driven by rate-of-return calculations and long-term capital gains (U.S. Bureau of the Census 2011). This is consistent with the reasons for ownership around the world, even though in the United States a larger percentage of housing stock is owned by corporations than in most other countries.

Larger properties are far more likely to accept subsidized tenants or to have subsidized units. Although larger properties' share of the overall rental market is approximately 30 percent, their share of subsidized housing is 60 percent.

Taxes

The taxing authority of the United States, the Internal Revenue Service (IRS), permits rental property expenses to be deducted from income. This includes expenses for maintenance, advertising, travel, management, legal, insurance, and other items necessary in managing the property.

Depreciation is a permitted deduction that is calculated not just on the property itself, but also on what is in and around the property. The real estate can be deducted over 27.5 or 40 years, depending on the method chosen. Fences built on the property, shrubbery, and roads are depreciated over 15 years. Automobiles, computer equipment, office equipment, and furniture have depreciation periods ranging from 5 to 10 years.

Property taxes are handled at the local level, and additional income taxes can be levied at both the state and local levels.

The IRS has different classifications for professionals who spend more than half of their time in real estate–related activities and for those who are part-time landlords. If there are losses on the property, active owners can deduct up to US$25,000 a year against their rental income, although unused deductions can be carried forward into another year. The deduction phases out as the owner's gross income increases.

Many small owners make only a minimum amount of income, enough to pay for expenses with a small amount left for profit. However, the depreciation deduction can cause losses, even though they are not cash losses. This creates a situation in which the property is paid for over time, and the owner gets an additional offset against income.

Financing

One factor makes financing for multifamily units different in the United States than in most other parts of the world: Buildings of up to four units can be financed through single-family mortgages, including with Federal Housing Administration (FHA) insurance. That means that more than 50 percent of the rental housing stock might not show up in multifamily financing statistics.

Financing for multifamily housing of properties with five or more units has been widely available in the United States. Between 1998 and 2008, the value of multifamily mortgages grew from US$430 billion to US$830 billion. However, lending slowed dramatically in 2009, not only because of overall tightening in the credit markets, but also because of an increase in delinquent or foreclosed loans. Interestingly, there was a significant difference in delinquency rates, depending on how the mortgage was financed. Those financed with commercial mortgage-backed securities saw a doubling in nonperforming loans, from about 7 percent in 2009 to 14 percent in 2010. Yet the number was only 5 percent for banks and thrifts and 1 percent or less for the Federal National Mortgage Association (Fannie Mae), the Federal Home Loan Mortgage Association (Freddie Mac), and FHA.

The growth in the multifamily finance market has been caused primarily by Fannie Mae, Freddie Mac and FHA. In 2011, FHA's total volume was approximately US$11 billion. The amount of units it insured tripled from

49,000 in 2008 to 150,000 in 2010. Fannie Mae and Freddie Mac's market share grew by 30 percent from the end of 2007 until 2010.

The example of the United States shows that finance can help to stimulate market growth, but economic conditions can also cause slowdowns. In general, finance has not been a barrier, particularly for small owners.

Subsidies

Even though the United States has traditionally had a vibrant real estate finance market, and even though its system of taxation is considered fair, there is still a large percentage of U.S. families for whom the market is not working. According to the Department of Housing and Urban Development (HUD), the number of those with worst-case housing needs grew by 42 percent in the past decade. Subsidies have addressed only a small portion of this need.

The United States has different types of subsidies for ongoing support for affordable housing. Tenant-based rental assistance is commonly known as a housing voucher.[15] In this assistance, a low-income or very-low-income family pays 30 percent of its income toward rent. The difference between this percentage and what is known as the "fair market rent" (FMR) is paid by the federal government. The FMR represents an apartment that would rent at the 40th percentile of the local housing market, based on an analysis of new leases from the previous year. In some cases, particularly in major urban areas, the FMR can set rents higher or lower than the specific market in which the apartment is located, because the FMR covers a wide geographic area and market-based rents reflect the particular submarket in which the unit is located.

In project-based rental assistance, the federal subsidy is tied to the unit itself, not to the tenant. This assistance provides funding to privately owned multifamily rental housing projects. To be eligible for the program, a participant must be a private owner and can be a for-profit or nonprofit organization, cooperative, a corporation or partnership, or other type of organizational structure (HUD 2012a).

Project-based rental assistance provides a guaranteed income stream to the owner. However, because the government sets the market rents based on its determination of fair market value, the rents were sometimes either too low to provide an incentive for keeping a unit in good repair, or too high, creating a drain on the federal government. In the cases of units that had FHA-insured loans, if the owner did not keep the property in good condition, the main tool would be to stop paying the subsidized portion of the rent. In this case, the reduction in cash flow could potentially force the property into foreclosure and thereby create an insurance claim.

Tenant-based rental assistance, whereas providing some degree of flexibility to tenants, generated years-long waiting lists in many major cities. In New York City, for instance, nearly 128,000 people were on the waiting list when the city closed its waiting lists to additional applicants. Moreover, a great many landlords will not participate in the program, causing a lack of good housing choices (Fernandez 2009).

Public housing, social housing that is owned and managed by government authorities, also plays a role in providing rental housing in the United States. Although public housing authorities (PHAs) manage public housing programs, they are technically not considered part of the federal government. They are creations of local and state jurisdictions and, generally, the chief executive of the municipality appoints the board of commissioners. The key programs to finance public housing are the public housing capital fund, which receives US$2.5 billion, or nearly 6 percent of the federal housing budget, and the public operating capital fund, which receives approximately 11 percent of the budget or just under US$5 billion.

Unfortunately, the capital needs of public housing are far greater than the resources. The 2013 budget submission by the president estimates that there is a backlog of US$18–22 billion of unmet modernization needs (HUD 2012b). One of the ways the government is trying to address this backlog is through the Capital Fund Financing Program. Here, the government permits each PHA to pledge up to one-third of the capital funds it expects to receive over the next 20 years. The lender or investor receives the funds directly from the federal government; they do not even pass through the PHA. The major risk here is appropriation risk—that Congress will not provide sufficient appropriations to make these payments. Given that it is unlikely that capital funds will be completely eliminated, the other properties in the housing authority's portfolio bear the risk. This is because the payments to the lender or investor are guaranteed. If the appropriations are reduced in the future, the PHA will have less on the balance of its portfolio.

For example, if a PHA expects to receive US$10 million per year in capital funds, it can pledge US$3.3 million to a lender or bondholder in exchange for a loan. Under current market conditions, the PHA can raise approximately US$37 million for modernization or new construction, assuming a 6.5 percent interest rate. If, in the future, the appropriations were cut by 50 percent to US$5 million, the lender would still receive the $3.3 million, but the PHA would have only US$1.7 million for its other properties (US$5 million minus US$3.3 million) versus US$6.7 million if the appropriations remain level.

To illustrate the challenges of public housing, we can look at Newark, New Jersey. Newark is significantly poorer than the United States as a whole and has a far greater percentage of renters.[16] The Newark Housing Authority, the 11th largest PHA in the United States, estimates that it needs approximately US$500 million to modernize its systems, yet it receives only approximately US$19 million annually in federal capital funds. Even if it were to pledge the full 33 percent of its capital funds, it would be able to raise only about US$71 million. Therefore, it will face some difficult choices in the future.

What the federal government is encouraging PHAs such as the Newark Housing Authority to do is twofold. First, it is asking that they evaluate the physical needs of the properties. When these needs are too great, PHAs can remove the most burdensome properties from their portfolio and give the tenants vouchers to find alternative housing. Second, the government encourages

Table 5.13 United States: HUD Budget, 2010

Category	US$ millions	Share of budget (%)
HUD budget 2010	43,581	100.00
Tenant-based assistance	18,184	41.72
Project-based assistance	8,552	19.62
Public housing capital fund	2,500	5.74
Public housing operating fund	4,775	10.96
Total	34,011	78.04

Source: HUD Fiscal Year 2010 Budget Summary.
Note: HUD = Department of Housing and Urban Development.

PHAs to find alternative sources of capital, such as the low-income housing tax credit program (LIHTC) (see box 3.5 in chapter 3).

The scope of assistance is still small relative to the need. Approximately 1.2 million families live in public housing, 1.3 million live in privately owned housing where the landlord receives the subsidy for the unit (project-based assistance), and approximately 2 million families receive vouchers to assist them with rental payments (tenant-based assistance). The three groups receiving these three types of subsidies represent only 3.9 percent of the U.S. population. When combined with other budgetary funds dedicated to public housing, such as capital funds and operating funds, nearly four-fifths (78 percent) of HUD's budget is dedicated to providing rental housing assistance and to operating and maintaining public housing (table 5.13).

Conclusion

The United States has many factors to create a vibrant rental market. Capital is available for multifamily finance, for both small and large owners. The tax system is considered fair. And rental housing is considered an acceptable alternative to home ownership. Yet the mortgage crisis and subsequent tightening of credit has put a great deal of pressure on rental markets. Vacancy rates are declining and rents are increasing. The percentage of those with rent burdens continues to rise—especially in large metropolitan areas and in areas that experienced the brunt of the financial crisis.

The U.S. system uses a combination of demand- and supply-side subsidies. Both the public and the private sector are actively involved. Unfortunately, the percentage of those receiving subsidies is quite small relative to the overall need, and subsidies can serve only a portion of the low-income market. Yet the United States still faces tremendous needs to add rental housing and to modernize the existing rental housing. Even with US$26 billion spent each year on housing subsidies, with more than US$7 billion spent on capital and operating subsidies for public housing, and all the investment stimulated through the LIHTC, this need continues to grow.

While the private market serves some of the rental population, public housing serves another portion, and subsidies are an important part of the U.S. system, many people still live in substandard housing. Although the United States has a multitude of public and private sector resources, obtaining good quality, affordable rental housing is still a challenge for many U.S. citizens.

Uruguay*

Housing and Rental Market

Based on the available data about housing stock, Uruguay appears to have a surplus of housing. This is distinct from most other countries in Latin America, which instead wrestle with an insufficient supply of housing units. In 2004, the population and housing census showed that there were about 1.28 million housing units, of which about 80 percent were permanently occupied. About 240,000 units were vacant for extended periods of time. Of these surplus units, about half were intentionally vacant for much of the year, such as vacation apartments in Punta del Este and other resorts. About 55,000, or approximately 5 percent of the total supply, were vacant for other reasons, such as being renovated or offered for sale or for rent. An additional 48,000 were vacant but not rented, many of which were in a deteriorated condition (INE 2011).[17]

The housing surplus is partly explained by recent demographic trends: the number of households was 1,062,000 in 2004, compared with 970,000 in 1996. This corresponds to a total increase of 91,000 households over eight years, while the housing stock increased by 150,000 units (50,000 occupied and 100,000 unoccupied) over the same period. In addition, there was net emigration estimated at between 120,000 and 150,000 persons. Housing demand has also been changing as a result of a reduction in the average size of households, an aging population, and population movements, including emigration. As a result of these factors and, especially, the gradual reduced density of urban Montevideo, an excess of housing units has accumulated in the urban core. Many of them are in poor condition.

Despite the surplus in housing, housing quality has become a serious bottleneck. Of units inhabited by low-income households, an estimated 90 percent need major repairs. The housing ministry estimates that there is a qualitative deficit of roughly 178,000 units, taking into account overcrowding, deterioration, and a lack of one or more basic services such as energy, water, or sanitation. Most of the vacant stock is dilapidated.

Unlike in most of Latin America, Uruguay's informal housing sector remains relatively small. There has been no history of major land invasions as occurred in Argentina, Brazil, Colombia, Mexico, or Peru. An estimated 11 percent of the population currently lives in informal settlements, in contrast to Colombia or Mexico where these rates reach up to 33 percent. However, this statistic depends on macroeconomic circumstances. For instance, after the country's banking crisis of 2002, the portion of the population housed in informal settlements grew at a rate of about 10 percent per year for several years. The increased growth of these

---

*The Uruguay case study was provided by Yoonhee Kim, Taimur Samad, and Claude Taffin.

Rental Housing · http://dx.doi.org/10.1596/978-0-8213-9655-1

settlements reflected a reduced delivery of low-cost units, reduced incomes, growing job insecurity, and increased informal employment.

Another characteristic of the housing sector is the relative prevalence of rental housing. The ownership rate is one of the lowest in Latin America—about 61.5 percent in 2004 according to the housing survey—while 15.2 percent of households were tenants. The remaining 23.3 percent were "occupiers" including various forms of informal housing. Whereas most informal occupants are low-income (in the fourth decile and below), tenants are mostly in the moderate and high-income brackets; 51 percent of them are in the sixth decile and above.

An important conclusion of this overview is that, unlike in many other countries in Latin America, renting seems to be an acceptable form of tenure in Uruguay. It could be an important policy tool for reaching the lowest-income families, provided that affordability issues for tenants are addressed and relevant incentives are supplied to investors.

Key Housing Policies

The government's support for housing has focused primarily on home ownership. The Ministry of Housing, Spatial Planning and Environment (MVOTMA) has three main tools:

- Purchase of existing units: MVOTMA supplies loans and grants funded by the National Fund for Housing and Urbanization (FNVyU) to finance the purchase of "economic units" by income-tested applicants with a minimum down payment.
- Housing cooperatives: MVOTMA provides loans and grants to housing cooperatives whose purpose is the construction of housing for their members. These cooperatives may operate under a system of savings and loan, under a mutual aid system, or under user or owner tenure.
- Housing production: MVOTMA produces housing units built through bidding procedures. In 2007, this agency helped arrange the construction of 1,600 homes in different *departamentos* (an administrative division below region level). The buyers are eligible for loans and grants from the FNVyU.

Given the importance of housing quality over mere quantity, a large share of government support is now focused on renovation. MVOTMA provides loans for renovation or expansion of owner occupied units that are funded by the FNVyU and include micro loans. In addition, the government provides housing allowances under which MVOTMA has implemented a system of subsidies to stabilize the housing circumstances for families belonging to housing cooperatives. The subsidy is the difference between the value of their share in the cooperative and 20 percent of the household income. Finally, the government also provides credits for materials to help improve the quality of lives of families with incomes below Ur$100; MVOTMA offers credit for building materials (CREDIMAT). The same incentive is available to those who want to expand, renovate, or build a house.

The only form of support to the rental sector is a rental guarantee, provided by the Rental Guarantee Fund (*Fondo de garantia de Alquileres*). This fund is designed to help households that can afford to pay rent but have no collateral or real guarantee. Except for this fund, there are no other major programs for rental housing. There are no other instruments that would create incentives for private investment in rental housing and no demand-side subsidies for low-income tenants, resulting in little investment in the formal rental market. A number of other factors may explain the absence of investors in rental housing:

- Although the regulatory environment for rental housing, such as tenant rights, appears to be satisfactory, there may be issues such as lengthy procedures or a lack of enforcement of court rulings by local authorities.
- The tax system is unfriendly, resulting in an uneven playing field with other forms of real estate or financial investments.
- Financial instruments, such as long-term loans and guarantees for lenders to invest in, do not exist for building new rental property or for renovating existing properties. Finance and management solutions are lacking for builders and investors in multifamily rental housing.

A policy reform and investment agenda should build on analysis of regulatory and market conditions in these key areas of reform.

Notes

1. The Ministry of Cities considers as being part of the housing deficit or backlog the units occupied by poor families (earning up to 3 minimum wages) paying more than 30 percent of their income for rent expenses. The official definition of the housing deficit includes other types of inadequate housing, like high-density and provisional housing.
2. Interview with Jaques Bushatsky, director for Rental at the Real Estate Association in São Paulo (SECOVI) on February 14, 2011.
3. Danwei (work units) was the basic organization in the old communist China.
4. "Deposits and Consignment Fund": a state-owned multifunctional financial institution controlled by the Parliament.
5. The "Housing 1 Percent" is a tax paid by private companies employing at least 20 persons; it now amounts to 0.45 percent (initially 1 percent).
6. Moreover, the basis for this ratio is 10–15 percent lower than the market value.
7. The stock in the former is highly fungible; in the latter, it is not.
8. The housing stock figures count the dwelling units on the basis of title ownership. This means that a row house consisting of eight inhabitable units counts as one dwelling if the whole building is registered under one name. If such units are counted by the number of inhabitable units, the 2010 housing stock figure is 17.67 million units.
9. Recently, INFONAVIT developed a program targeting some informally active categories (domestic employees, microentrepreneurs), who have yet to be registered in the social security system.

10. CONAVI (Comisión Nacional de Vivienda or the National Housing Commission) is a federal agency in charge of the implementation of the national housing policy.

11. The population numbers are as of 2010.

12. The total housing stock figure is from the 2010 population census, whereas the figures for HDB-controlled units and private residential dwellings are from the *Yearbook of Statistics 2010* (Department of Statistics). There is a small discrepancy in that the total stock figure is slightly larger than the sum of HDB units and the private housing stock.

13. Interviews at GH Bank, November 2010.

14. Douglas C. Yearley Jr., chief executive of Toll Brothers, in the *New York Times*, May 31, 2011. http://www.nytimes.com/2011/05/31/business/31housing.html.

15. This is one component of what is known as "Section 8" assistance. The other component is assistance that is tied to the unit, or project-based rental assistance.

16. The U.S. census shows Newark's share of renters at 74.7 percent compared with the nationwide share of 33.1 percent. Its per capita income is US$17,178 compared with US$27,041 nationwide. Some 21.1 percent of Newark's families live below the poverty line, more than double the national share of 9.9 percent.

17. All supply and population figures are from Plan Quinquenal de Vivienda 2005–09.

References

Abramo, Pedro. 2009. "Mercado imobiliário informal: a porta de entrada nas favelas brasileiras." In *Favela e mercado informal: a nova porta de entrada dos pobres nas cidades brasileiras*. Habitare: 4. Porto Alegre.

Amzallag, Michel, and Claude Taffin. 2010. *Le logement social*, 2nd ed. Paris: Collection Politiques locales, L.G.D.J. English version, *Social Rental Housing in France*. http://siteresources.worldbank.org/FINANCIALSECTOR.

ANIL. 2006. "Le logement locatif en Allemagne." *Habitat Actualité*. ANIL, Paris.

Belleza, Sérgio D. O. 2010. "Balanço anual dos fundos imobiliários 2010." FUNDO IMOBILIÁRIO—Consultoria de Investimentos Ltda, February 27. http://www.fundoimobiliario.com.br/rentabilidades.htm#.

Bonducki, Nabil Georges. 1998. *Origens da habitação social no Brasil. Arquitetura moderna, Lei do Inquilinato e difusão da casa própria*. São Paulo, Brazil: Estação Liberdade/Fapesp.

CGDD. 2012. Comptes du logement: Premiers résultats 2011; Le compte 2010. CGDD, La Défense. http://www.statistiques.developpement-durable.gouv.fr.

Chen, Jie. 2010. "On How to Deal with Vacant Housing in China." *Exploration and Free Views* 10: 57–60. (In Chinese)

CODI (Cooperative Organizations Development Institute). 2009a. "Annual Report." Bangkok, Thailand.

———. 2009b. "Workshop on Shelter Security and Social Protection for the Urban Poor and the Migrants in Asia." Ahmedabad, India, February 11–13.

Department of Statistics. 2010. *Yearbook of Statistics 2010*. Singapore: Ministry of Trade and Industry, Republic of Singapore.

Droste, Christiane, and Thomas Knorr-Siedows. 2011. "Social Housing in Germany— Changing Modes for a Changing Society." In *Social Housing Across Europe*, ed. Noémie Houard, 34–48. Paris: La Documentation française.

ElBoghdady, D. 2011. "Affordable Rental Housing Scarce in U.S., Study Finds." *Washington Post*, April 25. http://www.washingtonpost.com/business/economy/affordable-rental-housing-scarce-in-us-study-finds/2011/04/25/AFcBjilE_story.html.

Fernandez, Manny. 2009. "Thousands Lose Vouchers in Cutback." *New York Times*, December 17. http://www.nytimes.com/2009/12/18/nyregion/18vouchers.html.

Ghekière, Laurent. 2007. *Le développement du logement social dans l'Union Européenne. Quand l'intérêt général rencontre l'intérêt communautaire*. CECODHAS-USH-Dexia. Paris: Dexia Editions.

Global Property Guide. http://www.globalpropertyguide.com.

Huang, Yuxuan. 2010. "An Investigation into the Use of REITs to Finance Affordable Housing in Mainland China." Ph.D. thesis, Massachusetts Institute of Technology, Cambridge, MA.

HUD (U.S. Department of Housing and Urban Development). 2012a. "HUD's Public Housing Program." http://portal.hud.gov/hudportal/HUD?src=/topics/rental_assistance/phprog.

———. 2012b. "Public and Indian Housing, Public Housing Capital Fund, 2011 Summary Statement and Initiatives." http://hud.gov/offices/cfo/reports/2011/cjs/public-housing-cf2011.pdf.

INE (Instituto Nacional de Estadistica). 2011. Principales Resultados 2010; Encuesta Continua de Hogares. INE, Montevideo.

Joint Center for Housing Studies. 2009. *The State of the Nation's Housing 2009*. Cambridge, MA: Harvard University.

Kemp, Peter A., and Stefan Kofner. 2010. "Contrasting Varieties of Private Renting: England and Germany." *International Journal of Housing Policy* 10 (4): 379–98.

Kilsztajn, S., A. Rossbach, M. Carmo, G. Sugahara, E. Lopes, and L. Lima. 2009. "Aluguel e rendimento familiar no Brasil." *Revista de Economia Contemporânea* 113–34.

Kofner, Stefan. 2009. "The Framework of the Private Rental Housing Sector in Germany." Paper presented at the ENHR Working Group on Private Rented Sector Workshop, York, U.K., April 27–28.

Kohara, L. 2009. "Relação entre as condições de moradia e o desempenho escolar: estudo com crianças residents em cortiços." Ph.D. thesis, Universidade de São Paulo, São Paulo, Brazil. http://www.teses.usp.br/teses/disponiveis/16/16137/tde-10052010-155909/es.php.

Lum, Sau Kim. 2011. "Government Policy, Housing Finance and Housing Production in Singapore." In *Global Housing Markets: Crises, Policies, and Institutions*, ed. A. Bardhan, R. E. Edelstein, and C. Kroll, 421–46. Hoboken, NJ: John Wiley & Sons.

Man, Joyce Yanyun, Siqi Zheng, and Rongrong Ren. 2011. "China's Housing Policy and Housing Markets: Trends, Patterns, and Affordability." In *China's Housing Reforms and Outcomes*, ed. J. Y. Man, 3–18. Cambridge, MA: Lincoln Institute.

Ministério das Cidades, Secretaria Nacional de Habitação. 2009. *Déficit habitacional no Brasil 2007*. Brasília.

National Statistics Office, Korea. 2010. *2010 Census of Population and Housing*. Seoul.

National Statistics Office, Thailand. 2000. *Population and Housing Census 2000*. Bangkok.

Paes Manso, Bruno. 2009. "Aluguel mais caro de SP é de cortiço." *Jornal o estado de São Paulo*. March 10. http://www.estadao.com.br/estadaodehoje/20090412/not_imp353477,0.php.

Perera, Ranjith. 2005. *Rental Housing of the Low-Income Groups in Bangkok Metropolitan Area: A Study of the Existing Typology of Housing and Their Environmental Conditions.* Bangkok: National Housing Authority of Thailand.

Phang, Sock-Yong. 2005. "Household Income and Expenditures." Department of Statistics, Singapore.

———. 2007. "The Singapore Model of Housing and the Welfare State." In *Housing and the New Welfare State: Perspectives from East Asia and Europe,* ed. R. Groves, A. Murie, and C. Watson, 15–44. Hampshire, U.K.: Ashgate.

Presidência da República. 1991. Lei 8,245—Dispõe sobre a locação dos imóveis urbanos e os procedimentos a ela pertinentes. Brasília. http://www.planalto.gov.br/ccivil_03/Leis/L8245.htm.

Rappaport, Jordan. 2010. "The Effectiveness of Homeownership in Building Wealth." Federal Reserve Bank of Kansas City, Kansas City, MO. http://KansasCityFed.org.

Rothman, Andy, and Julia Zhu. 2011. "Food, Flats and the Party." *China Strategy,* CLSA, May.

Fundación CIDOC and Sociedad Hipotecaria Federal (SHF). 2009. *Estado Actual de la Vivienda en México 2009.* México City: table 7, page 43, using ENIGH 2008 data.

Streitfeld, David. 2011. "Bottom May be Near for Slide in Housing." *New York Times,* June 1. http://www.nytimes.com/2011/06/01/business/01housing.html.

Ulrich, Jing, Amir Hoosain, and Kelvin Wong. 2011. "China's Affordable Housing Program: Picking up Momentum." Hands-on China Report, JP Morgan.

UN-HABITAT (United Nations Human Settlements Programme). 2003. *Rental Housing: An Essential Option for the Urban Poor in Developing Countries.* Nairobi: UN-HABITAT.

U.S. Bureau of the Census. 2011. *Property Owners and Managers Survey, 1995.* http://www.census.gov/hhes/www/housing/poms/overview.html, last revised September 30.

———. 2012. American Community Survey. http://www.census.gov/acs/www/.

Wu, Jing, Joseph Gyourko, and Yongheng Deng. 2012. "Evaluating Conditions in Major Chinese Housing Markets." *Regional Science and Urban Economics* 42 (3): 531–43.

Yap, Kioe-Sheng. 1996. "Low Income Housing in a Rapidly Expanding Urban Economy: Bangkok." *Third World Planning Review* 18 (3): 307–23.

Environmental Benefits Statement

The World Bank is committed to reducing its environmental footprint. In support of this commitment, the Office of the Publisher leverages electronic publishing options and print-on-demand technology, which is located in regional hubs worldwide. Together, these initiatives enable print runs to be lowered and shipping distances decreased, resulting in reduced paper consumption, chemical use, greenhouse gas emissions, and waste.

The Office of the Publisher follows the recommended standards for paper use set by the Green Press Initiative. Whenever possible, books are printed on 50% to 100% postconsumer recycled paper, and at least 50% of the fiber in our book paper is either unbleached or bleached using Totally Chlorine Free (TCF), Processed Chlorine Free (PCF), or Enhanced Elemental Chlorine Free (EECF) processes.

More information about the Bank's environmental philosophy can be found at http://crinfo.worldbank.org/crinfo/environmental_responsibility/index.html.

green press INITIATIVE

www.ingramcontent.com/pod-product-compliance
Lightning Source LLC
Chambersburg PA
CBHW081505200326
41518CB00015B/2383